ID0966542

"I have long admired Dick DeVos and his family for the values they stand for. I have known Dick ever since he spent time with the Cowboys as a high school football player. In football, successful players are only free to perform their best when they understand the courage and conviction needed to 'do the right thing.' This principle also applies to life. As Dick so convincingly argues here, we cannot enjoy true freedom unless we have the courage to live by the values he speaks to. This book is not only inspiring, it is a must read for anyone interested in the future of our country."

—Tom Landry, former coach, Dallas Cowboys

"*Rediscovering American Values* shows how our freedom depends on our ability and willingness to act with virtue. This book provides a much-needed guide to Americans, perplexed by the fraying of our social fabric, who want to rebuild the ordered, moral lives that are necessary for prosperity and happiness, both for the individual and for the community."

—Spencer Abraham, U.S. senator

"I'm super enthused about this book! It was waiting to be written—and Dick DeVos was just the right person in America to write it! Buy it! Read it!"

—Robert H. Schuller, Crystal Cathedral

"In this timely volume, Dick DeVos builds his argument for the maintenance of freedom in the United States upon the uncontested foundation of moral righteousness. The values which he so clearly delineates—by means of carefully selected real-life examples—echo the scriptural premise that 'where the Spirit of the Lord is, there is liberty.' Every concerned citizen would profit by reading and reapplying this catalog of values as elucidated by one of America's most outstanding Christian businessmen."

—D. James Kennedy, Ph.D., senior minister,
Coral Ridge Presbyterian Church

"Instead of grimly chronicling the decline of American values, Dick DeVos has drawn a colorful road map to their restoration. This practical and convincing volume, from a business leader who knows what works and has proven it, will guide you at work and at home while it banishes despair and fills you with buoyancy and hope."

—Rabbi Daniel Lapin, author of *Toward Tradition*

"Dick DeVos has learned from his father a deep love of freedom and a clear understanding of the traditional American values that make our freedom possible. There is as much wisdom in this inspirational book as in the speeches of George Washington and Ronald Reagan."

—Edwin J. Feulner, Jr., president, Heritage Foundation

"Dick DeVos has written a powerful book about American values and what those values demand of each of us. Those values are written large across our history, but their true meaning comes alive only in the stories of men and women whose faith and character have turned, and are still turning, the stuff of dreams into the very fiber of freedom. Those stories are here, and from their lessons we learn anew what America's future can be."

—Gary Bauer, president, Family Research Council

"Dick DeVos has written a foundational book, loaded with common sense, rich in examples and illustrations that are simple in concept and profound in their application. It's an excellent guide for daily living."

—Zig Ziglar, author of *Over the Top*

"A beautiful tribute to the enduring principles and values that have made and will continue to make this country great well into the next century. An inspiring, introspective work that powerfully salutes the moral fiber of our American quilt."

—Stephen R. Covey, author of
*The Seven Habits of Highly Effective People*

"*Rediscovering American Values* makes the case for time-honored principles like courage, honesty, perseverance, humility, self-discipline, and compassion. Dick DeVos provides practical advice and real-world examples of what it takes to remain a free and decent nation."

—William J. Bennett

"The message in *Rediscovering American Values* comes straight from the heart, and it takes a man who lives by these values to write sincerely about them. With passion, humor, and common sense, DeVos tells a wonderful story about America and about the ideals that hold us together and keep us free. This is a truly inspiring book."

—John Engler, governor of Michigan

"America is on the verge of a new awakening. When we have stumbled or fallen in the past, we have not only picked ourselves up but have found the inner strength to reach new heights. Dick DeVos recognizes this, and that's why his perceptive, well-written book is so timely and so well worth reading."

—Steve Forbes

"Wonderfully inspiring and motivating. Dick DeVos has identified the greatest challenge to our country as we approach the millenium: reinvigorating those values which set us apart. This is the message America needs."

—Chuck Colson, chairman, Prison Fellowship

# Rediscovering American Values

The Foundations of Our
Freedom for the 21st Century

DICK DEVOS

WITH A FOREWORD BY PRESIDENT GERALD R. FORD

A DUTTON BOOK

DUTTON
Published by the Penguin Group
Penguin Putnam Inc., 375 Hudson Street, New York, New York 10014, U.S.A.
Penguin Books Ltd, 27 Wrights Lane, London W8 5TZ, England
Penguin Books Australia Ltd, Ringwood, Victoria, Australia
Penguin Books Canada Ltd, 10 Alcorn Avenue, Toronto, Ontario,
Canada M4V 3B2
Penguin Books (N.Z.) Ltd, 182–190 Wairau Road, Auckland 10, New Zealand

Penguin Books Ltd, Registered Offices:
Harmondsworth, Middlesex, England

First published by Dutton, an imprint of Dutton Signet,
a member of Penguin Putnam Inc.

First Printing, September, 1997
10   9   8

 REGISTERED TRADEMARK—MARCA REGISTRADA

LIBRARY OF CONGRESS CATALOGING-IN-PUBLICATION DATA:

DeVos, Dick.
    Rediscovering American values : the foundations of our freedom for the
21st century / Dick DeVos.
        p.    cm.
    ISBN 0-525-94227-0 (acid free)
    1. National characteristics, American.   2. Social values—United States.
3. United States—Politics and government—Philosophy.   I. Title.
E169.1.D475   1997                                                        97-15190
306'.0973—dc21                                                               CIP

Printed in the United States of America
Set in New Baskerville
Designed by Jesse Cohen

This book is printed on acid-free paper.  ∞

All of the author's proceeds from the sale of this book go to the
Compassionate Capitalism Foundation.

*To my wife, Betsy, whom I love with
all my heart, and to our four children,
for it is they, and all our children,
who hold the keys to our future.*

# Contents

## PART III—PRESERVING FREEDOM:
### Helping Others to Do the Same

# Foreword
## by President Gerald R. Ford

At the end of a century scarred by war and darkened by oppression, the world looks to America for a new birth of freedom. For the first time in memory, the human family is no longer divided by hateful walls or brutal ideologies. We have stepped back from the narrow window ledge of nuclear confrontation. And the winds of freedom blow, from the Moscow city council to the formerly one-party states of eastern Europe, Asia, and Africa.

If, as I believe, Americans have a missionary role to play, then freedom is our gospel. Freedom to vote and freedom to worship. Freedom to think for ourselves and freedom to influence the thinking of others. Freedom to demand change and freedom to resist such demands. Yet, while freedom is universally desired, it is individually defined. For some it is freedom from intrusive government. For others, it is the freedom to pursue long-delayed hopes, sometimes with government as a necessary ally.

In the post–Cold War world, the leadership we seek is moral rather than military. For we recognize that the empires of tomorrow will take shape, not on traditional battlefields, but in living rooms and church pews, research labs and teaching halls. Amid so much that is changing, it is all the more crucial for Americans to cling to values that are changeless—to honesty and compassion, fairness and decency. For in this age of dizzying technological advances, we need inspiration as much as information, and faith to match our facts.

Why do free societies disperse their leadership? In part because they distrust concentrated power but also because they have faith in the extraordinary qualities to be found within seemingly ordinary men and women. Free men and women work hard, aim high, and give back to the community more than they take out of it. Some may hold public office, but many more serve the public in positions of civic and business responsibility.

With their feet on the ground and their eyes on the stars, grassroots leaders everywhere are busy shaping the next American century around the conviction that liberty is a gift from God, not government. Because they know that one man or woman, fired by an idea and free to pursue his or her dreams, can make history, even while making a profit.

Dick DeVos is such a dreamer. I have known Dick since he was a youngster working summers at his father's small soap factory in Ada, Michigan. Growing up, Dick gained a sense of place, optimism that he was part of a moral universe, and the guiding belief that we are members of the same family. The world has turned over many times since then. Today's Amway is one of the largest family-owned businesses in America, and a shining example of capitalism with a conscience. And the young man I first knew in Ada is an international entrepreneur overseeing operations in over forty countries, with annual sales of more than six billion dollars.

Dick has succeeded as a husband and father, as the president of a great worldwide company, as a leader in the community, and, more recently, as an economic statesman of global stature. All this makes him eminently qualified to help us regain an appreciation for freedom here, in the "land of the free." We've all heard the old saying "Nice guys finish last." Dick refutes that somewhat cynical notion every day of his life and on every page that follows.

Perhaps more than any other company I know, Amway embodies the personal work ethic. At the same time, Dick DeVos recognizes that society holds the ultimate franchise on our talents. He has never made the mistake of measuring success in purely material terms. For him, life is judged a success not by what you get but by what you give.

No doubt Dick has been given many wonderful opportunities. But if he has made the most of what has come his way, it is because of his character, not his name. He is both a visionary and, if I might use the term, a *throwback*—a throwback to an earlier time, when a man's word was his bond and business could be conducted with a handshake. Today, when lack of trust in our governing institutions is a bipartisan problem, Dick reminds us that the genius of the Founders was to create a society governed from the bottom up, not dictated to from the top down.

With ideals but without illusions, he suggests how modern society can shed its skin without losing its soul. Free government, as he is quick to point out, does not mean no government at all. Our nation came into being as an experiment in self-government. That means self-regulation: personal, economic, social, and political. It takes integrity to regulate ourselves in a way that upholds freedom.

In bold and original ways, Dick describes how values such as honesty, self-discipline, initiative, and brotherhood create the very foundation upon which freedom and the free-enterprise system rest. The America he describes will ensure more opportunity, not less, for each succeeding generation.

More than 170 years ago, an elderly gentleman in Quincy, Massachusetts, wrote to his friend atop a Virginia mountaintop. John Adams, then in his eightieth year, wanted to know whether seventy-three-year-old Thomas Jefferson would be willing to live his life over again. Jefferson replied promptly and positively. For he believed the world to be a good place, one where pleasure outweighed pain. "My temperament is sanguine," he added. "I steer my bark with Hope in the head, leaving Fear astern. My hopes indeed sometimes fail, but not oftener than the forebodings of the gloomy."

I've never heard a better definition of what it means to be an American. Like a runner nearing the end of his course, I hand the baton off to those, like Dick DeVos, who share my hopes for the future and my reverence for a country that has never become but is always in the act of becoming. After all, presidents come and go. But principles endure, to inspire leaders yet unborn. Here freedom's lamp burns bright. And by that light, we can all find our way home.

# Introduction

I was twelve years old when my parents put me to work at their small soap factory in Ada, Michigan. For thirty-five cents an hour I was responsible for watering the lawns and weeding the flower beds. At that time, my father, Rich DeVos, and his partner, Jay Van Andel, were busy building their company. Yet no matter how busy Dad seemed to be, he was always there for me with an encouraging smile and the kind of attention that made me feel special, even though I was one of four children. His praise for a job well done filled me with pride. I didn't realize it at the time, but through those simple tasks I was being taught the values upon which our great country was built—the values that uphold the very freedom that we hold so dear. This book is about those values and that freedom.

You may ask why a busy executive would want to take time

out to write a book. The truth is, I felt compelled to do so. Traveling the world, I witness again and again mounting concerns over issues of morals and values, and confusion surrounding matters of right and wrong. In the midst of this, as a Christian, as a husband and father, and as a businessman and an American, I feel that I have gained a perspective on life that may be helpful to others. My hope is that somewhere here you will find experiences and insights that resonate. I also hope that you will find the ideas challenging and inspiring. They might even confirm what you already know.

Essentially, this book is about freedom, and the values that provide the foundation of freedom. I was fortunate to be born into an environment that provided me with extraordinary opportunities to learn about the values behind freedom—and the tremendous results that occur when they are properly applied. I had inspired teachers and great examples to follow, the most important being my parents, Helen and Rich DeVos. I was also blessed with a set of "backup" parents, Betty and Jay Van Andel, my parents' friends and business partners.

Dad and "Uncle Jay" began their business life together in the DeVos and Van Andel family basements in 1959. Five years later they moved their factory to a converted gas station on Fulton Street in southeast Grand Rapids. While Dad and Uncle Jay were immensely proud of their factory, my brother Dan and I were happy because this meant we finally got our own bedrooms!

Before Amway outgrew our home, my mother hosted business meetings, filled product orders, and cooked meals for distributors in addition to caring for her young and growing family. A high school student printed our product literature, and the family laundry room doubled as the shipping department in the afternoons. Despite the hectic pace of life, however, my parents always made time to say a prayer before each meal, to discuss school activities, and to crowd together on our thirty-five-year-old sailboat for weekends on Lake Michigan.

In spite of the challenges and frustrations of building a business, our small crew never lost faith in God and the values He taught us. When I say values, I mean the principles we hold in our hearts and minds that shape who we are, how we live, and how we treat one another. For my family, those values were the same ones admired by our country's founding fathers and that have traditionally supported and upheld freedom and free enterprise in our nation. Dad and Jay held these values in such high esteem and were so proud of their country's heritage that they named their first distributor organization the American Way Association. This eventually led to the creation of the Amway name.

In a now famous speech, "Selling America," which Dad first delivered in the early days of Amway, he championed all that was right and good about our nation and the free-enterprise system on which its economic prosperity was built. This message so impressed then-Congressman Gerald Ford that he read the entire speech into the U.S. *Congressional Record.* It has been reprinted, and taped versions have been replayed many times since.

Dad and his partner did everything they could to help people achieve their own American dream. Amway distributors don't work for Amway. They work for themselves, operating their own Amway businesses. The more Dad talked about Amway's approach to business, the more people listened, and the more they saw the potential for themselves and their families through building and owning an Amway business. In the years that followed, Dad, Jay, and thousands of Amway distributors succeeded far beyond their own dreams and expectations.

By the age of sixteen I had left the lawn-maintenance crew and had become one of Amway's three tour guides. To avoid complications, I didn't introduce myself as Dick DeVos but used my middle name, Marvin. As Dick Marvin, I thoroughly enjoyed taking groups through our plant. I had a lot of fun when I was asked such questions as whether I had ever met Rich and Jay and, if so, what they were really like. I could honestly say that I had met them both and that they were very supportive and encouraging, even to a part-time tour guide like me.

By the time I had graduated from our local public high school, our product line had expanded from laundry detergent to furniture polish, oven cleaner, housewares, and cosmetics. Amway now had 200,000 distributors, and the number of employees was approaching 1,500. Annual revenue had exceeded $150 million, and the company had expanded to two countries outside of North America: Australia and the United Kingdom.

After my first few months at a local college I realized that the family business held a great deal more interest for me than biology and chemistry, so I left school and took on a full-time position at Amway, as a liaison between the still-growing company and its distributors. I began to work to build what would become lasting relationships with distributors.

Being the boss's son obviously had its advantages, but it also meant I had to work extra hard to earn respect. At least that's how it seemed to a skinny teenager trying to keep up with the adults. But I didn't mind. My parents continued to encourage me to trust my instincts, to discover and use fully my God-given talents, and to be the unique individual God created me to be.

I soon learned that one of my abilities was working with people. Perhaps it was for this reason that I got my first promotion. As a member of the Amway "travel team," I took on the job of traveling the country, making presentations to distributor groups and meetings. I had to gather, synthesize, and communicate a variety of information on the company, its marketing plan, and its products. Looking back, I realize that this took a great deal of initiative, self-discipline, hard work, and courage—qualities that did not come naturally or easily to a nineteen-year-old.

But I loved what I was doing and was soon offered the position of a travel-team manager. Around this time, Dad and Jay began to take a more serious look at the involvement of the four DeVos and four Van Andel children in the business. They decided that before any of us could assume management responsibilities, we would each have to experience, firsthand, every aspect of the business. I'm not sure I would have so readily agreed to this process had I known that it would take the next six years of my life. However, I have to confess that what I learned during this time was invaluable.

Dad and Jay taught me to put people first, even if this meant making short-term sacrifices, which I later realized were always for the long-range good. Amway is first and foremost a people business. Employees were often encouraged to bring their spouses to company functions. Family members of employees were given hiring preference. Distributors were encouraged to develop their businesses as husband-and-wife teams.

I believe that the net result of this "family friendly" approach, which was so very innovative at the time, was the development of a high degree of loyalty and trust among Amway employees, Amway distributors, and the founding families. It's no wonder—given this emphasis on family—that Dad and Jay were frequently invited to attend baptisms, weddings, and bar mitzvahs. They considered this an honor, not a chore.

One of the weddings that Dad attended during this time was my own. I was twenty-three years old and had fallen in love with beautiful Betsy Prince of Holland, Michigan, who shared my Dutch heritage as well as my Christian commitment.

Meanwhile, my management training gave me a thorough introduction to each department of the Amway Corporation. The training did not involve just observation, but was also very much hands-on. I did everything from running errands for Research and Development to driving forklifts and loading trucks, working on production lines, running tabulations in accounting, buying paper for our printing operations, and driving an eighteen-wheeler. There were no special privileges for me. I had to follow all the rules and meet all the standards. In order to drive the forklift, for example, I had to take safety training and obtain a special license, just like any other Amway employee.

At a certain point, despite a heavy work schedule, I decided it was time to get my college degree, and so, in conjunction with Northwood University, I combined independent study with weekend classes to complete my bachelor of business administration degree.

During my early hands-on training program at Amway there was a learning experience to be had in every department I worked in. For instance, in Research and Development, I got to see the value of committing to a vision, taking initiative, and persevering. I found it interesting that while R and D had excellent scientists on the payroll, many good ideas came out of the mailbags full of letters from distributors, homemakers, and other users of our products. These letters contained ideas on everything from cosmetic applicators to electrical generators. Distributors and customers still send us letters. They write because they know that our company respects their concerns, listens to their ideas, and is committed to excellence in all that we do.

As a result of that commitment to excellence, I became aware of the increasing role that technology would play in the future of our expanding company. I learned that automation didn't replace people; it set them free to concentrate on tasks that were less repetitive and more intellectually stimulating and productive. In fact, by remaining competitive through automation, the business grew so much that Amway had to hire even more people to keep up with demand.

In a very important part of my management training, Betsy and I also became Amway distributors, experiencing firsthand how the values of the manufacturing company translated from the plant floor into the homes and lives of our distributors and customers. I saw that the quality of our products had a direct impact on the lives and environment of the people who used them. Since its inception, Amway had the distinction of being one of the first companies to produce and sell biodegradable cleaning products worldwide. In fact all our cleaning products were biodegradable, highly concentrated, produced without fillers, and packaged in an environmentally compatible fashion. All of this combined to reduce any pollution caused when consumers used the products. And by producing products without fillers we were able not only to cut back on shipping costs, but to use less of our country's precious natural resources as well. The leadership role that Amway played here—years before "ecology" had become a household word—made a real difference to our customers, not to mention the environment.

From both my upbringing and my Amway work experience I observed another important lesson: My father's word was his bond. I know it may sound like an old-fashioned concept, but my father, his partner, and their company lived up to the agreements that they made, even when it cost them dearly to do so. Their business was built on trust, the result of their honesty and reliability. A handshake or a spoken promise had the same value as a signature. In fact, the contractor who built the majority of the Amway complex never had a written contract, because he never thought it was necessary. Distributors understood this too, and they in turn passed it on to their growing number of new distributors and customers. This same trust remains today as the most valuable asset at Amway.

Following my completion of the training program and another assignment working with our distributors in North America, I was promoted to corporate vice president of Amway International. This gave me my first taste of the qualities that successful upper management must exhibit on an ongoing basis. And I got a taste of the responsibility they must shoulder. As vice president I was responsible for operations in eleven different countries and for developing strategies that would help us expand into many more. Because international sales were only approximately fifteen percent of Amway's total sales at that time, it was an exciting growth opportunity.

I made another important discovery as I worked on expanding Amway abroad: The same values that I had learned to champion at home were just as effective and meaningful overseas. What worked in Keokuk, Iowa, and Friendship, Maine, also worked in Fremantle, Australia, and Kawasaki, Japan. How exciting it was to see people in other nations, many of them exercising economic freedom for the first time, embracing values held dear by Americans, applying those values to their own lives and businesses, and flourishing as a result. By the end of my approximately six-year tenure as vice president of Amway International, sales from outside of North America had tripled to become more than half of Amway's total global revenues, and Amway had expanded from eleven to eighteen international markets.

My family's entrepreneurial spirit must have finally kicked in, for at the end of this tenure I left Amway to launch my own independent management company, with Betsy as my partner. I went from being an executive at what had become a giant international corporation to being president and hands-on manager of the day-to-day, on-the-edge operations of a variety of small businesses that were struggling to get started or stay competitive. It is said that small-boat sailors can advance to big boats, but the reverse is difficult. While a big boat will heel in a gust, the same wind can capsize a small boat. I had to learn to react quickly to forces that would hardly be felt at a big company, but could quickly sink a small business. I learned in a very personal way what risk really feels like. Without the large corporation's crew of specialists to advise me, I had to develop many new skills.

This was a remarkable period of growth for me. I had the challenge of building a company of my own in a working relationship with my wife, helping raise a family, participating in church activities, and pursuing my civic responsibilities, which included election to the State Board of Education in Michigan. I also had the opportunity to serve as president and CEO of an NBA basketball team, the Orlando Magic, which my family purchased in 1991.

In the course of meeting these challenges, I began to study and analyze those values—now shaped and tempered by my life experiences—that had so well served the DeVos and Van Andel families through years of great challenge and growth. I didn't pursue this study as an academic exercise but rather as the key to my survival and ultimate success. Those values gave me the confidence to step out of my father's very large shadow to pursue my own interests and to return later to make my own unique contribution to the family business.

Had Dad not experienced a mild stroke in the summer of 1992, I would have been content to work with Betsy, raise our children, and operate our own business-management company. But at the request of my dad and siblings—and with a certain amount of trepidation—I returned to Amway and prepared to succeed my father as president, to follow a man who was and is a living legend there.

My return to Amway was made more difficult when just prior to the announcement of Dad's retirement, he suffered a major heart attack. Thankfully he recovered after extensive hospitalization, but with limitations on his activity level.

Nonetheless, I took the reins and proceeded on the principal conviction that the key to productivity and future growth was the unleashing of the creativity, talents, and energies of Amway people—both employees and distributors—not just the centralized and single-minded pursuit of efficiency. I took the view that profits were not our immediate goal but would be the natural and appropriate outcome of doing everything else right. To reinforce our company's sense of partnership, we encouraged employees and distributors to work cooperatively and to be truly accountable for their particular part of our operation.

I saw it as my role to make us a truly global company, sharing our products, values, and vision with the rest of the world. Together, we found new and better ways of expanding our global presence, constantly testing our products, vision, and values in new environments. Headquarters were still in Ada, Michigan, but I know Amway distributors who took part in pulling down the Berlin Wall, helped to oust a corrupt dictator in Panama, and came to the rescue of Florida residents in the wake of Hurricane Hugo. Just as the telecommunications revolution was creating an information highway accessible to anyone, Amway was creating a global, human highway that promotes entrepreneurship, free enterprise, and what my father calls Compassionate Capitalism.

While many of America's leading manufacturers proclaimed that Japanese markets were closed to U.S. companies, Japan was embracing the spirit of our way of doing business. Now, in fact, Amway sales in Japan are approaching two billion dollars annually, ranking us as one of the top-performing foreign companies in Japan. And the same government that sent soldiers into Tiananmen Square has welcomed the manufacturing and sale of Amway products in mainland China, taking what I hope is an important step toward future freedom and opportunity in that country. In less than four decades since its founding, Amway has come to represent more than two and a half million independent Amway distributors in more than seventy countries and territories, and to generate over six billion dollars in sales per year.

In mid-1995, Steve Van Andel took over his father's position as chairman. Having grown up with Steve, I now have the privilege of working with him. Not only is he a very capable businessman, but we share the same values as well—the same values reflected in this book.

While some may think the co-founders' or now Steve's and my leadership is responsible for Amway's amazing achievement, the fact is, it's not one or two who make a company successful—it's many people working together, sharing common values and a common vision for the future. As my father has said many times, our company is about people helping people help themselves. That is a very large part of our success. It's something all our distributors and employees can be proud of. And I know they are.

As I look to the future, I see that the values that built America, that built the Amway business, and with which I was raised are now more important than ever, not just for our company but for our nation and its people. These are values that can transform our government, reform our institutions, and strengthen our families. They are values that go beyond mere legal and ethical constraints and that must be on our minds and the minds of all citizens and leaders alike. Such values as honesty, humility, reliability, cooperation, perseverance, and accountability must also be taught to our children, for they are the values upon which our personal, civil, and political freedoms rest. And as you will see in this book, these are values that do not stand alone. They must work together, tempering and supporting one another.

Like my dad, I am an optimist. I love my country. It pains me when I hear critics say that American businesses can't compete on a global level, that our leaders are morally bankrupt, and that our nation's best years are behind us. Despite increasing global competition, American companies *can* compete and win in the global marketplace. I know because I've been a part of making it happen. American schools and colleges *can* be the finest in the world. I know, because I've worked with high-quality teachers and administrators and I've hired their graduates. Government *can* be responsive to the needs of its citizens. It's already happening in Grand Rapids, Michigan, and in hundreds of other cities and small towns across the nation.

However, before our nation can fulfill its destiny—to truly become the land of the free—all Americans must understand what freedom means. To do that, we must understand the values that provide the very foundation of freedom. As we talk about these values in the following pages, you will meet contemporary American heroes from all walks of life who have applied these values in their lives.

Because of my own background and my current role as president of Amway, my experiences with the company inevitably serve as an important frame of reference. However, this is not a book about Amway, its employees, or its distributors. Indeed, there are many wonderful and inspiring Amway tales to be told, but the illustrations I have chosen come from a broader pool. Some of the stories may be familiar. Many will not. But all of the people in these stories have contributed to greater freedom in America.

Above all, this book is a call to challenge our comfortable assumptions and to rediscover the values that have been the very soul and conscience of our nation's freedom.

# PART I

# UPHOLDING FREEDOM:
## Doing What Is Right

Thomas Jefferson, the great framer of our Declaration of Independence, said, "God, who gave us life gave us liberty. And can the liberties of a nation be thought secure when we have removed their firm basis?"

No one knew better than the men and women who founded our great land of democracy that freedom is possible only when it is rooted and grounded. For many, freedom conjures up the image of a flag blowing freely in the breeze or a kite soaring unfettered, high in the sky. Yet without a flagpole to anchor it, a flag will blow away, and without a tether to earth, a kite will come crashing to the ground.

I learned a long time ago that freedom doesn't mean just getting away with doing whatever we want, whenever and however we want to do it. Like the flag and the kite, our freedom must be anchored to certain values; otherwise, freedom drifts away into moral decay or comes crashing down in the dust of tyranny. If we hope to sustain the spirit of freedom and opportunity for which our country stands, we need to rediscover those values—the principles upon which America was built and for which countless of its citizens have given their lives.

The range of choices available to individuals depends upon the level of freedom a society affords. However, the level of freedom society can provide depends, in turn, upon the individual choices that its citizens make. The more "right" choices individuals make, the more freedom we will have. The more "wrong" choices individuals make, the less freedom we will have.

As soon as we say this, of course, we run the risk of raising hackles. Any statement that includes the word "right" is bound to upset someone. Many people today believe that there are no universal rights and wrongs—that what is right for one person is not necessarily right for another. Others say that we can do what we want as long as we don't hurt anyone else. I believe we have to say, "We can do what we want as long as we do what is right."

"Doing what we want as long as we do what is right" may sound like the ultimate catch-22. It's saying that freedom means we can do what we want. But it's also saying that we must do what is right, which may not necessarily be our immediate desire. So how do we know what is right, and how do we make ourselves do it?

Dr. Alan Keyes, a former ambassador, maintains that the moral courage that built America is the true foundation of our freedom: "The men and women who first launched the great experiment in liberty we enjoy to this day did not tell us that freedom would be an easy road. They offered us a hard-won vision for the future of America." In other words, it takes will and courage to make ourselves do what is right.

To answer the first question—How do we know what is right?—I believe that all people have an intuitive sense, a consciousness, of right and wrong. It's an integral part of human nature. Personally, I believe this ability to discern between right and wrong comes from our Creator. I believe that God has provided us with a moral blueprint, and our conscience is the vehicle for understanding that blueprint and for receiving divine guidance. But regardless of where you believe our sense of right and wrong comes from, if you believe that freedom is a human birthright, then you have to agree that what supports, upholds, and protects that freedom is right, and what diminishes it is wrong.

The question that naturally arises is, "Who should do the upholding?" Do we guide and determine our own behavior, or does the government take that responsibility? My grandfather helped me answer this question when he once asked me, "Do you want to limit your own arm swinging when you are about to hit someone in the nose, or do you want to call in the arm-swinging police?"

Although government clearly plays an essential role in upholding the freedom and rights of individuals by creating laws and enforcing them, the reality is that the more government involvement or intervention is required, the less freedom all of us enjoy. Certainly the preferable means of control, whenever possible, is our own free will. Human dignity is better preserved when we restrain ourselves rather than having restraints imposed upon us by laws and law enforcement agencies.

If we are to exercise our free will to do what is right, however, we have to know what is right. And how do we know what is right? From what source do we receive our guidance? For me, as a Christian, that is easily answered. I ask myself, "What would Jesus do?" I even wear a bracelet woven with the letters WWJD as a ready, daily reminder to apply that question in my life situations. But whatever your personal beliefs, you must seek moral guidance and direction if you do not want government to take control of every detail of your life.

Our founding fathers had great appreciation for and understanding of the necessity of this need for guidance from within. They called this guidance from within "virtues," which can also be labeled morals, principles, or values. I have come to regard those values that help us uphold the freedom and rights of others—"to do what is right"—as components of one overarching quality, "integrity."

The word "integrity" comes from the Latin root *integrare*, which means to make whole. It is also defined as "a firm adherence to a code, especially of moral values." And in my view, true integrity requires the working combination of not just one or two values, but at least eight, all of which are important and interdependent: honesty, reliability, fairness, compassion, courage, humility, reason, and self-discipline.

If we understand and properly apply these values to our

lives, both personally and in society, we will be able to uphold the spirit of freedom and opportunity for which this country stands, and America will continue to be the world leader it was destined to be.

# 1

# Honesty

Do you remember the first time you were dishonest? As a boy, I certainly got burned enough trying to lie or mislead others to the point of dishonesty.

Honesty, the first and perhaps the most important component of integrity, can easily be seen or described as "telling the truth"—that is, keeping our words consistent with our thoughts. Honesty also involves consistency between our thoughts and our actions. Earlier we said that integrity is a firm adherence to a code of moral values and, from the Latin derivative, "a state of being complete or undivided." Thus, men and women of integrity are not divided; they maintain consistency among their thoughts, words, and actions. They do not compartmentalize their lives, applying one set of values in one situation and another set of values in a different situation.

In the Judeo-Christian tradition, honesty is fundamental to God's law, which commands us "not to bear false witness." But a person doesn't have to be either Jewish or Christian to see the lasting and immutable value of honesty. Society cannot exist or function properly when people aren't honest. When everything is subject to question—when everything is questionable, doubtful, or suspicious—the system goes awry.

Our words and actions connect us, whether through a long-distance satellite transmission or a firm handshake. Every important decision we make assumes honesty on the part of those involved. For example, my decision to marry my wife, Betsy, was based on our honest sharing of love, faith, and commitment. Another important example might be a decision to have surgery. When we make such a decision, we are depending on the honesty of the surgeon who recommends it. Honesty, however, goes far beyond our own personal decisions. It affects other people as well.

I am reminded of the much-admired golf champion who once disqualified herself from a tournament because she hit the wrong ball out of the rough. When a friend later said to her, "Nobody would have known," the golfer replied, "But I would have known." This woman clearly understood that her honesty or dishonesty regarding only one golf stroke affected more than her own standing. Because of her honesty, the trophy belonged to somebody else.

For many of us, myself included, the hard lessons of honesty begin on the playing field. Not surprisingly, then, the spirit of honesty exhibited by the golf champion is also captured in a series of events involving a young baseball player who put honesty above winning.

The story was first reported in Florida newspapers, for the

game took place in a small town outside of Palm Beach. The game was T-ball, and the oldest player was seven years old.

The game was well under way when first baseman Tanner Munsey fielded a ground ball and tried to tag a runner on his way to second base. Laura Benson, the umpire, called the runner out. But Tanner approached Benson and confessed that he hadn't actually tagged the runner.

"I missed him," said Munsey, and Benson reversed her call.

At the end of the game, Tanner's coach dusted off the game ball and presented it to the boy as a reward for his honesty.

The story doesn't end there, though. Two weeks later, in another game, Tanner was playing shortstop when a similar play occurred. This time, however, Benson, who was again the umpire, called the runner safe. The look on Tanner's face immediately told the umpire that the boy thought she had made a bad call.

"Did you tag him out?" Benson asked.

"Yes," said Tanner. And despite the initial protests of the opposing coach, Benson reversed her call.

Because Tanner had been honest in the previous situation, honoring the right of the other player to have what he had honestly earned, the right to stay on second base, the umpire trusted Tanner in this situation and gave him what he had earned, tagging the runner out. Tanner's integrity had earned him the trust of the umpire.

"If a kid is that honest," she said to the coach, "I have to give it to him."

It's perhaps something of an indictment of the state of our nation that a story like this would be considered news. But the fact is, the story was even picked up by *Sports Illus-*

*trated.* Everyone loves a good sport, and good sportsmanship requires honesty.

There is probably not a society on earth that does not value honesty. Yet all of us, at some time, have very likely been burned by our own dishonesty. For myself, I am still learning to be honest about my own time limitations. It's hard for me to say no, so I tend to overcommit myself, which occasionally prevents me from doing all that I could and should be doing to fulfill my commitments.

Actually, being honest is the easiest course of action, although it may not seem that way initially. Dishonesty in difficult circumstances just produces an increasing web of deception that creates more difficulty later on. As the old saying goes, "It's easy to tell a lie, but hard to tell just one." And pretty soon it is hard to remember where the truth ends and the fiction begins. Besides, I learned early on that the negative consequences of honesty are always better than the negative consequences of dishonesty.

A dishonest person abuses today's trust at the expense of tomorrow's. While dishonest people have only the thin veneer of their lies for support, honest people have the confidence of truth to support them. They have the true freedom that comes when what they say and what they do are consistent.

We all know what dishonest behavior is: it includes stealing, cheating, exaggerating, false flattery, telling partial truths, twisting the truth, making promises we do not intend to keep, lying to protect ourselves from appropriate consequences, and lying to gain control of others or to put them at an unfair disadvantage.

But dishonesty can also be withholding information that

is important to another, particularly if that information is required to make an informed decision. People who are not told the truth cannot make good decisions. In fact, they can be led to make incorrect conclusions. Every day, we base decisions on assumptions of honesty. This can be readily seen in something as simple and basic as a road sign. If the expressway sign indicates that the road goes to Philadelphia, we expect it to take us to Philadelphia, not New York.

Honesty is not always easy, though. It requires diligence and daily practice—sometimes despite overwhelming temptation. This was certainly true for Tom and Pauline Nichter of Buena Park, California.

Tom had lost his job at a warehouse the year before, and Pauline had recently been laid off when her employer, a large national credit-card company, closed her division. The family had been forced to sell some of their belongings and move into a tiny room in the modest home of Pauline's parents. For lack of storage space, they kept many of their remaining personal possessions in their car.

One evening, Tom and Pauline and their eleven-year-old son, Jason, were driving past the Buena Park Mall when Jason suggested that they stop at the mall. Tom was reluctant to stop. He had only seventy-five cents in his pocket, which he intended to use to buy a can of chili for the family's dinner. Tom hated to have to tell his son that he could only window-shop, but the boy's persistence finally won him over. He parked the car, and the three of them went into the mall.

One of Jason's favorite places in the mall was the Kay-Bee toy store. While her son looked at the toys, Pauline browsed at the front of the store. She was looking at some items near the cash register when she noticed an oversized gray leather folder lying on top of a stack of games. She could clearly see that there was money inside. At first she thought it was play money, but when she took a closer look, she discovered that the money was real. At a guess, she thought the folder contained $200 to $300 in cash.

Pauline was overjoyed. It seemed to her that the good Lord was providing for them in their time of need. After giving the matter more thought, however, and discussing it with Tom, she realized that God hadn't given them the money. He might have entrusted them with it, but the money belonged to someone else. Not to attempt to find the owner would be dishonest.

Tom and Pauline took the folder to the mall's police sub-station, but it had already closed for the night, so they drove to the nearby Buena Park police station. There, Pauline placed the gray folder on the counter and told the officer on duty where she had found it. When the officer examined the folder, he found that it contained far more than Pauline had suspected. Inside were credit cards, a passport, a $1,500 plane ticket, and $2,394 in cash!

The officer on duty called the Buena Park Mall information center to advise them of the discovery, and minutes later a very grateful tourist arrived to redeem his lost property. He thanked Pauline and her family profusely.

The Nichters did not ask for a reward, nor was one offered. They did, however, accept the $3 the Buena Park Police Department gave them to buy hamburgers.

There might have been no more to this story had a KNBC reporter not been at the police station that night. He saw

Pauline return the money and thought her honesty deserved mention on the evening news.

No sooner was the story broadcast on television than the police station switchboard lit up with calls from viewers expressing their goodwill toward Tom and Pauline. Within days, letters and postcards began arriving for the Nichters, addressed to the Buena Park police station. Then an anonymous donor walked into the station, asked how much money had been returned, and wrote a check to Pauline Nichter for $2,400.

"It's the least they deserve," said the donor.

Tom and Pauline were surprised and overwhelmed when the police came to their door with the sack of letters and the check. But that was just the beginning. A real-estate agent contacted Tom and Pauline and offered them the use of a small apartment until they got back on their feet, which, as it turned out, did not take long. A receiving manager in a raw-materials warehouse read the newspaper account of Pauline's honesty and gave her a job. Tom also received a job offer, which he gratefully accepted.

"There are plenty of people out there with good job skills," said one of the potential employers. "But I want someone I can also count on to do the right thing."

Our founding fathers understood that honesty is essential to democracy—that life, liberty, and the pursuit of happiness are impossible without the honesty of our country's citizens.

The last sentence of the Declaration of Independence contains the words "a firm reliance on the protection of Divine Providence." The drafters of this document recognized God's ruling hand in human action. Their belief in this higher form of law is what carries the moral imperative for all of us as citizens to do what is right. This is the "true" foundation of our God-given rights to life, liberty, and the pursuit of happiness.

# 2

# Reliability

R eliability, the second component of integrity, turns honesty into action, and it is a direct result of consistency between our words and actions. People who are reliable do what they say they will do. They keep their word. A phrase I like to use is "Trust equals consistency over time." People who are inconsistent become untrustworthy and, therefore, are considered unreliable.

Reliability is a good, solid value to be cherished, encouraged, and rewarded. The most obvious and easily understood form of reliability is punctuality and dependability in our work—which means consistently showing up and doing whatever we have agreed to do to the best of our ability. Individuals of integrity are reliable, whether they are auto mechanics, bus drivers, doctors, businesspeople, short-order cooks, or ballplayers.

One man who is famous for this kind of reliability is Cal Ripken Jr., the baseball player with the Baltimore Orioles who broke Lou Gehrig's fifty-six-year-old record by playing in 2,131 consecutive games. Little wonder that he's known affectionately in the sport as "the Iron Man."

For this accomplishment, Ripken was voted "Sportsman of the Year" by *Sports Illustrated* magazine. His story, carried by all the media, was a welcome respite from the dark cynicism that seemed to have overtaken this favorite American pastime following acrimonious negotiations and a lengthy strike that eventually forced cancellation of the World Series.

I think it's quite an accomplishment, given this atmosphere, that one man singlehandedly turned the attitudes of millions of sports fans from declining interest to adulation, and even renewed fervor for major league baseball. Especially since Ripken is the kind of man who quietly and politely— but firmly—walked away from a *People* magazine photo shoot that was running overtime because he had a commitment to pick up his daughter from school.

Ripken's rise to prominence was founded on the basics, which he learned from his father, a former coach for the Baltimore Orioles. As the family traveled the circuit, Cal got to practice his plays with many of the soon-to-be greats and journeyman players of the day. He gained great respect for the game of baseball and became dedicated to its craft.

This served him well, since he did not begin his career as a standout player. Baseball scouts saw little more in him than competence. Far from being vaulted into the limelight upon his entry into the big leagues, he found eight other shortstops picked ahead of him in the 1978 baseball draft.

Over the years, however, he distinguished himself as a

good, solid shortstop, earning the American League Rookie of the Year Award. But the single most distinctive quality that ultimately made him a contender for the Hall of Fame is that Ripken played every game he could, as well as he could.

That kind of reliability is worthy of note in any profession, but some reporters covering Ripken's achievement said that no one should be lionized just for showing up to work on a regular basis. I strongly disagree. Ripken was justly honored. Reliability in and of itself is a worthy accomplishment and deserving of attention. In addition to "just" showing up, however, Ripken continued to distinguish himself by the quality of the job he did. I'm sure many a "young tiger" challenged him each spring for his starting position, but the combination of his reliability in being there and his giving his very best gave him the winning edge.

Work that we agree to do, or a title that we accept, implies certain promises and responsibilities; it says that we know what we are doing in our particular field of work and will do a competent job of it. If someone calls himself an accountant but consistently makes errors, he is unreliable. While he might be an honest person, his incompetence lessens his reliability and thus his integrity.

Similarly, if an employer were to fire an otherwise loyal and hardworking employee for making one minor mistake, that employer would soon gain a reputation for being unreliable. Reliable people act rationally, or with reason, and not in an arbitrary and potentially unfair manner.

Good communication also plays a part in reliability. If we do not adequately communicate with others about what we mean or what we intend to do, we become unreliable. Reliable people communicate appropriate information in a timely manner.

American workers often demonstrate extraordinary reliability by going beyond the call of duty, allowing their employers to count on them even in the most challenging situations or times. H. B. Fuller of St. Paul, Minnesota, the largest independent manufacturer of adhesives and sealants, discovered this when one of their employees won admiration for the company by paying close attention to her customers. Lorinda Tucker, a secretary in Fuller's Louisville, Kentucky, office, illustrates this aspect of reliability at its best.

A potential customer in Macon, Georgia, had called Tucker's boss about problems he was having with a type of glue he was using for a specialized operation. He wanted to know if H. B. Fuller had a product available, "right now," that could be used instead. The customer's need was urgent, but Tucker's boss was out of the country and the local Fuller salesman was on vacation. In many cases, an employee who received such a call under such circumstances would have taken the message and let the matter wait for the boss's return. But Lorinda Tucker went the extra distance.

She began by contacting her company's regional technical service center in Greensboro, North Carolina, and describing the problem to them. The service center determined which of the company's seven thousand adhesives, sealants, and coating formulations would fit this customer's needs. The only stock on hand, however, happened to be right there in Tucker's hometown, Louisville. Mindful of the time factor, she drove her own pickup to the product warehouse, loaded up five hundred pounds of the product, and took it to the airport. There she learned that the freight company that linked Louisville and Macon had a flight scheduled to leave in thirty minutes, but H. B. Fuller didn't have an account with the airline and the bill was going to be close to three hundred dollars. Tucker solved the problem by going to a nearby automated teller machine and withdrawing money from her personal account.

The result was nothing short of spectacular. A few hours after the original emergency call had been placed, the material was in Macon, Georgia, and was being loaded onto the customer's production line. Not only did the production line run uninterrupted, but it operated better than it had before because the new adhesive outperformed the one the company had purchased from the other supplier.

To many, Tucker's actions might seem remarkable. But there is nothing miraculous about them—except for the fact that going the extra distance is not something everyone will do.

Reliability is important in business, both in our products and in our relationships with our customers and employees. The economies of free markets and free nations are based upon this reliability.

One hallmark of Amway's products is reliability. We have a one hundred percent money-back, satisfaction guarantee on everything we sell. Any of our customers can receive their money back for products they may find unsatisfactory. But we can back this up only because our employees who produce those products are reliable. And as a manager, I know that I must be reliable if people are going to work for me and be effective. To do their best, they must be willing to take reasonable risks, knowing they can rely on me to support them in both their successes and their failures. If they cease to take such action and initiative, the whole system breaks down.

We need more reliability in our world today—in every area of life. Take, for example, the political arena, where there is an increasing trend toward saying whatever one needs to say to get elected, without the willingness—the reliability—to follow through on those promises. This has led to voter cynicism and loss of faith in our political process.

One politician for whom I have great admiration is John Engler, the governor of Michigan. His recent reelection campaign theme was "Promises made, promises kept," and he did just that. Although his popularity declined during his first term, he would always say: Don't read the polls. Let's just do what we said we were going to do. Let's fulfill our commitments. Even those who disagree with Governor Engler acknowledge his reliability. For instance, he promised to balance Michigan's budget, and in 1996 he proudly signed the fifth consecutive balanced budget. He also promised to cut taxes, and, as of this writing, taxes have been cut twenty-one times since he took office.

The results of our actions are strongly influenced by the consistency between our actions and our words. This kind of reliability demonstrates that inner moral compass, that blueprint we hold to, even when faced with external pressures to do otherwise. And when we are reliable, we provide a strong foundation upon which others can base their own decisions. In doing so, we better uphold their freedom.

# 3

# Fairness

Fairness, the third basic component of integrity, means consistently putting self-interest, bias, or prejudice aside and holding the same standards for everyone. By its very definition, fairness is a form of justice, which relates to both civil and human rights.

For the purposes of this book I am not going to discuss justice as it applies to laws or the legal system. What I am going to cover is justice or fairness as it is applied in "the golden rule"—treating others as we want to be treated.

The Bible says that all human beings are created by and in the image of God. This is also stated in our Declaration of Independence. Our founding fathers understood this and preserved our freedom by stating, "We hold these truths to be self-evident, that all men are created equal. They are endowed by their Creator with certain unalienable Rights, that among these are Life, Liberty and the pursuit of Happiness." I find that this belief strengthens my own ability to honor others and to uphold their freedoms as strongly as I do my own. When it comes to being fair to others, the most valuable rule we can apply is the age-old golden rule: "Do unto others as you would have others do unto you." I think of this every time I look at my "What Would Jesus Do?" bracelet.

Robert George, the former CEO of the Medallion Construction Company in Merrimack, New Hampshire, is a businessman who tried to consistently apply that rule. Like all of us, he faced the issues of fairness on a daily basis. And like all of us, his ability to behave in a fair and upright manner was not easy. All too often the problem involved deciding on how to be fair to his clients, subcontractors, employees, and himself—all at the same time.

George invariably found himself needing to turn to the golden rule. In fact, maintaining that "ethical edge," which he believed distinguished his company, required George to apply the golden rule to everything he did, although he admits it was difficult—especially in a company that employed over a thousand people in three different states. Acting fairly can sometimes mean incurring short-term financial losses or letting an opportunity slip by. In the long run, however, George believed that the dividends were not only a good reputation and peace of mind, but financial as well.

In a story first reported in *Nation's Business* magazine, George described a challenge he faced when a subcontractor gave him a bid that George believed contained an error and was too low. At the time, Medallion Construction was a primary contender for a $2.5 million public-housing contract. This particular local subcontractor submitted a bid for electrical work that was 20 percent lower than George expected, and nearly $30,000 below the quotes of the four other subcontractors.

George's dilemma might have been a difficult one if he had not been a man of integrity. If he accepted the bid, his own company would undoubtedly come in with the best price and would surely win the contract. Yet it was clear that the subcontractor had made an error that would cause him to lose money, and there was a strong chance that it might also result in putting him out of business.

"There wasn't a lot of time to decide," said George. "In this business, subs deliver their estimates just a few hours before the primary contractor must submit his bid, so you don't have time to play one subcontractor against another."

George realized it would be unfair not to bring the error to the attention of the subcontractor. So he called the man and told him about the mistake, being careful not to disclose information that could hurt the other bidders. The subcontractor promptly withdrew his bid.

Medallion got the contract anyway, but that's not the end of the story. A year later, the same subcontractor submitted another low bid to Medallion. It was so low, in fact, that George was almost guaranteed to get the contract on which he was bidding. When he called the subcontractor, once again wanting to alert him to a possible error, he was told that the subcontractor was offering George a discount in return for his fair dealings in the past.

When we stop to consider the impact our decisions and actions have on others, as did Robert George, we are being fair to them. This does not mean that we compromise our integrity by accommodating some deliberate wrongdoing on the part of others. It does mean that we give people an even break, treating them as we would like to be treated.

Every life situation in which we find ourselves involves many conditions outside our control. But with our free will we can control our actions, as well as our reaction to those conditions, by making the right choices. When we choose an action, we also choose a consequence or reward, either by virtue of natural law, or by virtue of the law of nature's God. To be fair, we must allow others to reap the rewards of the actions that they choose. Similarly, we must allow them to reap the consequences.

Being fair also means respecting others, no matter where they are in life and no matter how far they might have fallen. In this regard, respecting others can sometimes require encouraging them to seek higher standards than they have been holding for themselves.

It was this kind of fairness that brought about a remarkable series of events on one of North America's largest Indian reservations. As a Native American storyteller describes it, Andy and Phyllis Chelsea, both residents of this reservation, had such a strong sense of fairness and respect for themselves and their people that they brought about an astonishing transformation—not only in themselves but in the entire community.

Imagine a rural community of four hundred people where alcoholism is epidemic, touching practically every man, woman, and child, often with devastating results. Imagine a dismal place where poverty, isolation, and idleness create an atmosphere of utter despair.

That was Alkali Lake, a Shuswap Indian village and the center of life on the Alkali Lake Reserve. The remoteness of this village nestled in the piney foothills of south-central

British Columbia, Canada, made it vulnerable to long-term neglect. Its isolation assured that its concerns would be relegated to a back burner by government agencies and all but ignored by private-sector philanthropies.

On the Alkali Lake Reserve in particular, the alcoholism rate was a staggering ninety-eight percent. Those who couldn't afford cheap wine, the preferred drink, would settle for beer, or, in a pinch, gasoline mixed with orange juice. Stumbling along from one government assistance check to the next, nearly everyone was chronically unemployed, sick, drunk, or all three. Unemployment and health problems have come to be regarded as endemic to reservation life, but even for a remote Indian reserve, ninety-eight percent was a devastatingly high proportion. It's little wonder the locals christened Alkali Lake "Alcohol Lake."

The prospects for the residents were as predictable as they were grim: automobile accidents, brawls, murder, sexual abuse, neglect, serious medical difficulties, high suicide rates, and early death. Death often came from something as simple as people drunkenly wandering outside into subzero weather to relieve themselves, becoming disoriented, and freezing to death.

Even more disturbing than the suffering among the adult population of Alkali Lake was the devastating effect alcoholism had on the children, who were often abandoned and had to fend for themselves for periods of days in the uninsulated, ramshackle hovels that served as their homes. In at least one instance, a small child was found nearly frozen to death under a pile of dirty laundry where he had sought refuge from the freezing temperatures.

Prenatal care was sporadic or nonexistent. Infants, often premature and struggling with a host of medical complications, were frequently born "passed-out drunk," their mother's amniotic fluid reeking of alcohol. The presence of fetal alcohol syndrome was astronomically high.

This was the situation when Andy and Phyllis Chelsea decided to stop drinking.

Phyllis was the first to take this stand. Her decision came as a result of an event involving her eight-year-old daughter, Ivy. Phyllis had literally gone off and forgotten where she had left her child. When this happened, Phyllis realized she had gotten to the point where her lack of respect for herself was endangering her children's well-being. It was then that she gave her children her solemn oath that she would either stop drinking, or she would let them go to a better life elsewhere.

Phyllis did stop drinking that day, though no one, including herself, was sure how long her resolve would last. Less than two weeks later, her husband, Andy, stopped too, and together they resolved to help each other turn their lives around.

At first their only goal was to change their own lives, knowing that would be challenge enough. And challenge only mildly characterizes what they eventually had to face.

In a strange but predictable reversal of social mores, the entire Chelsea family was initially ostracized from the community for their sobriety. But the stubbornness that had gained Andy a reputation as a tenacious brawler made him downright bullheaded about his sobriety. The more people insisted that he drink, the less he wanted to. And Phyllis dared not even consider risking the personal cost of drinking again, given her contract with her children.

Soon startling things began to happen as a result of their decision and follow-through. As one of the few sober men on the reserve, Andy was soon enlisted by the tribal council to serve out the term of the elected chief, who was moving to another province. At the time, the position of chief involved mostly ceremonial duties and was not envied by many.

Andy had his own agenda in mind, however. He accepted the position and immediately began to institute sweeping policy changes and controversial programs that only exacerbated the resentment the community had developed toward him and his family.

One of his most controversial moves was to have the monthly government aid checks channeled directly through his office. He then issued scrip that was good only for nonalcoholic supplies from the local markets. Next, he set alcohol-abuse treatment as the preconditon for receiving any financial aid at all.

In response to the implementation of this policy, Andy's erstwhile best friend, Freddie Johnson, threatened to shoot him. After a tense standoff, Freddie backed down, but for several anxious moments, the outcome was anything but certain.

In an effort to cut off the supply of alcohol entering the reserve, Andy and Phyllis then organized a sting operation in conjunction with the police against local bootleggers. From that operation, a list of offenders was drafted and shared with authorities. Those on the list were warned that they would be prosecuted to the full extent of the law if they ever violated the federal alcohol laws again. Andy's mother was on that list.

Over a period of a few years, the number of threats against the Chelseas declined, and a few of their old friends even started showing up at their home, looking for help and support in their efforts to stop drinking. Phyllis helped these people find the treatment they needed, often paying their travel and medical expenses herself.

When there were enough sober people to lend a hand, the Chelseas began organizing construction and cleaning crews to rebuild, repair, insulate, and furnish homes and to stock the larders of tribal members who agreed to go to alcoholism treatment programs. Tribal members had to go off the reservation to take part in these programs, so the Chelseas personally saw to it that children were properly fed and cared for in their parents' absence.

Treatment was not always voluntary. In especially difficult cases, particularly where children's safety was at issue, the Chelseas went to court and had the children legally removed from their parents' custody until the parents agreed to treatment. Phyllis often took the point position on these actions, heading up an intervention group that would confront the drinkers in their homes and inform them of their limited options.

But treatment in off-reserve clinics was not enough. There needed to be a local source of support, encouragement, and information. To fill this need, the Chelseas found a drug and alcoholism counselor, a Catholic brother named Ed Lynch, who set up and started a local Alcoholics Anonymous program right in the village and staffed it for many years.

Once a dilapidated shantytown, Alkali Lake is now composed of neat, secure homes and several new buildings that house an agricultural co-op, a day care center, a library, and a well-equipped bilingual school. The income once used to buy alcohol, and the building grants available to those sober enough to seek them, provided the funding. The school's headmaster is Freddie Johnson—the same man who nearly shot it out with Andy years before.

Of the many successful projects and enterprises undertaken by the Chelseas over the years, none speaks louder than the fact that thirteen years after Andy and Phyllis stopped drinking, the Alkali Lake community was officially ninety-five percent in recovery. And while not all of the problems of reservation life were solved, the community's way of dealing with those problems was vastly improved.

Both Andy and Phyllis attribute their success to their firm belief in the real dignity of each member of the tribe, regardless of their condition. One might argue that the Chelseas were not fair and did not respect their townspeople's right to free choice when they took such strong measures to get them off alcohol. I disagree. I believe that they fully respected their choices by holding them accountable for those choices and that they were being totally fair by not shielding them from the full consequences of their actions. They also respected the potential of their community members, even when it was impossible to respect the dependent alcoholics they had become.

The necessity for fairness also extended to the other people in their community. Being fair to others includes acting responsibly and holding ourselves accountable for our own actions. It includes doing our best to meet our own needs instead of demanding things from others.

Fairness can mean providing opportunities for others whenever possible. We are acting with fairness when we respect others' rights to flourish and to make the best possible use of their abilities, and when we give them fair and reasonable compensation for work done, recognizing their talents, encouraging the development of their abilities, and rewarding them for their efforts. It also means doing our best to ensure that the needs of others are met, whether it is in their marriage, job, friendships, or associations. Fairness also includes honoring policies and procedures that have been set and agreed upon by a larger group we are a part of, whether we personally agree with them or not.

Fairness can mean showing consideration by calling a spouse to say that we will be home late, or simply remembering to use our automobile's turn signal before making a turn. It is honoring someone by speaking directly to him and not behind his back, or listening when our children, spouse, friends, or co-workers have something they want to share with us.

At Amway, groups of our employees meet on a regular basis in sessions we call "Speak Up."

We instituted these regular meetings so that we could find out how we are doing, to seek feedback, and to better ensure that we are treating our employees fairly when it comes to compensation and benefits. Our intention is to create an environment of trust, openness, and fairness, and therefore we will not tolerate reprisals against any employee for bringing up issues.

Being fair to others is also being timely in communication and in exchanging ideas, information, and feelings that others need to know about. It is making sure our employees are properly and regularly informed about the business they are a part of. Our "Speak Up" sessions give us opportunities to talk about decisions that have been made. While fairness should not be confused with pleasing everyone or with everyone being in total agreement, it is fair to discuss decisions and to explain the rationale behind them. And we believe that if we are fair with our employees, they will be fair with us.

Finally, being fair is treating people with civility. Judith Martin, author of the syndicated column "Miss Manners," has said that proper etiquette, or civility, historically precedes law as a restraint of individual behavior for the common good, and is the oldest "deterrent to violence after fear of retaliation." This echoes the sentiments of the eighteenth-century English statesman Edmund Burke, who said that "manners are of more importance than laws."

By manners or civility, I do not necessarily mean the formal rules of etiquette. Instead, I am referring to respect for the feelings, ideas, and opinions of others (upon which many rules of etiquette are actually based). Our Constitution guarantees freedom of speech, which protects our individual right to express our opinions. Despite what many seem to think—and act out—freedom of speech was not intended to encourage people to be verbally abusive, to put others down, or to use destructive and inflammatory language. While the Constitution certainly allows us to do this if we want to, it is not the right thing to do.

In America, the only nation whose official founding documents define and protect its citizens' rights, civility and fairness are required if we as citizens are to respect the rights of others, treating them consistently just the way we want to be treated ourselves. What a way to honor each other.

# 4

# Compassion

Compassion, the fourth component of integrity, means "to suffer with." It is to feel sympathy or empathy for someone and to have the desire to help end his or her suffering or to alleviate its causes. Compassion strengthens our integrity by giving us the desire to do what is right.

For this reason, compassion is central to any definition of integrity. To me, compassion results in simply wanting the best for others. It is less an act of the intellect than an expression of the heart. Although our expression of compassion will differ from subject to subject, goodwill toward all is one natural outcome of this value.

Crucial to this, though, is our perception of others. I believe that the compassion we are able to feel for others grows in direct proportion to our own ability to understand that we are all created equal. If a person truly attempts to think about another's situation—to look at their present circumstances, their past, and the pressures they face—it is easier to imagine what it must be like to be in their situation, and thus to be more compassionate. And once a person can imagine being in someone else's shoes, compassion comes more naturally.

This becomes readily apparent when one looks at societies where there are ruling classes and underclasses. In general, the members of the ruling classes tend to show great and genuine compassion for each other, yet are devoid of any feeling for those in another class, even to the point of subjecting them to torturously inhumane treatment.

For Buddhists, compassion is one of the four unlimited states leading to nirvana. For Christians and many others, Jesus provides the best example of compassion in action, whether he was healing the sick or feeding the hungry. As the Bible says, "Administer true justice; show mercy and compassion to one another." The two greatest commandments are "to love the Lord our God with all our hearts, souls, minds, and strength" and "to love our neighbors as ourselves."

As stated earlier, this lies at the very heart of our Declaration of Independence, which states clearly where our rights come from: "We hold these truths to be self-evident, that all men are created equal, that they are endowed by their Creator with certain unalienable Rights." When we remember that all human beings were created equal by God, compassion comes more readily, because, in essence, we are recognizing our similarities as God's creations.

Recognizing our similarities to others also increases the likelihood that we will compassionately uphold their rights.

When others are vilified, villainized, or objectified, they are dehumanized. This takes away any basis for compassion, which is one reason why I so strenuously object to stereotyping races, nationalities, or sexes.

This necessity for seeing all people as human and equal was well understood by Dr. Martin Luther King, whom I admire greatly for his devotion to advancing the rights and freedoms of all peoples. In Dr. King's famous "I Have a Dream" speech, he challenged us that someday all people in America would be judged by "the content of their character and not the color of their skin."

People who think that compassion is nothing more than self-interest disguised as altruism are mistaken. Recent studies on philanthropy and volunteerism support what I know in my heart and have personally experienced: that we Americans truly have the capacity to act in the best interest of others, without regard to our own reward. Our country abounds with people who do good deeds for others, on a regular basis, without consideration for themselves.

However, this doesn't mean that everyone has the same capacity to feel compassion or to act upon their concern. Unfortunately, throughout our culture, compassion seems to be exhibited less and less on a daily basis, possibly because there is so little left to actually nourish or encourage it.

There is less human interaction than ever before. What interaction does occur is more likely to be a brief encounter with a stranger at the checkout line, or the person sitting next to us on the train or plane, or a keyboard connection on the World Wide Web. Rarely do children join friends and walk to school. Mom or Dad drops them off at school or the day care center. Children who take buses to school often attend schools far outside their own neighborhoods and have no classmates to play with who live within walking distance of their home. In many communities, neighbors, in the truest sense of the word, no longer exist. People may live next door, but they often are only names on mailboxes. With the increasing mobility of our society, families sometimes do not live in the same place long enough to make deep and lasting friendships possible. Television has taken people off their front porches and cocooned them inside. Long-term exposure to senseless violence and sexual exploitation on television and in movies also serves to numb them to the realities and challenges that real people face. The net result is isolation, detachment, loneliness, and a loss of compassion.

What has been lost, however, can be regained. If we understand the important role that compassion plays in our society, we will want to reclaim it—and we can. By "loving our neighbors as we love ourselves," we can restore a more compassionate society. From that comes the will to uphold the freedom and rights of others—the will "to do what is right."

This understanding could well be what has inspired the organizers of MADD—Mothers Against Drunk Driving—to run monthly gatherings known as "victim impact panels." As reported in the *Los Angeles Times,* at least twenty Los Angeles county judges regularly augment sentences for DUI (driving under the influence) by requiring offenders to attend these panels to meet victims of drunk drivers.

At one such monthly gathering, there were 250 "guests," all first-time offenders. Jan St. Michel was the first to take her place at the podium, displaying photos of her nineteen-year-old daughter, Robin, before and after the accident that had killed her. "Here's my little angel, lying in a hospital bed, tubes in her nose, tubes in her head," Jan said, showing a picture of her daughter when she was in a coma.

Robin had been driving home from a Fourth of July party when a drunk driver rammed into her car. The man had already consumed a six-pack of beer and was on his way to buy another. Jan described the hours of waiting while doctors tried to save her daughter's life. When she finally saw Robin, she was on life-support systems. Jan wept as she told the audience how she had sat at Robin's side, holding her hand, for two days before the life-support systems were removed and Robin took her last breath. As Jan shared her pain, grief, and loss, several listeners who had begun the evening with anxious joking or looks of boredom now sat motionless or wiped away tears.

The next speaker was Michele Sapper, a pale, slightly disfigured woman in her thirties, who moved slowly to the podium. She displayed a blown-up photo of a slim, tanned young woman with a beautiful smile. In labored speech, she said, "That was me before the accident."

Michele was a twenty-year-old college junior destined for graduate studies in child psychology when she was hit head-on by a one-ton pickup truck. The drunk driver didn't even put on his brakes as he careened out of control, dragging her car onto the front lawn of a house. The impact smashed her brain into her skull and sent her into a coma that lasted two months. Much to the surprise of her doctors, Michele learned to walk again, although it is still difficult. But her short-term memory is limited, and she suffers coma-inducing seizures. "I had a very exciting future that lay ahead, or so I thought," Michele told the group. "Because of somebody's irresponsibility that will never occur." As Michele spoke, she looked out at her audience. Many, unable to look back, gazed down at their laps.

Iris Giorgi spoke next. Her two grown daughters were on their way out of a hockey game when a drunk driver, ignoring traffic police, drove right into the crowd of fans on a crosswalk. Iris's older daughter, Lynnmaria, seeing the car racing toward them, tried to push her sister, Sandra, out of the way. She then tried to jump up on the hood of the car. But two other pedestrians had already been flung there and Lynnmaria was sucked under the car instead. When the car finally came to a stop, she was still trapped under it. A group of fans had to lift the car to get her out.

Lynnmaria lost her left ear and parts of her scalp, both her lungs were collapsed, three of her vertebrae were fractured, her bladder was crushed, and she had a spiral fracture of her left arm.

When Iris and her husband reached the hospital, no one knew what had happened to their younger daughter, Sandra. It was while they were waiting with Lynnmaria that the news came that Sandra was in a hospital miles away. She had suffered a fractured pelvis and massive head injuries. According to emergency-room doctors, she had to be resuscitated twice.

Iris Giorgi went on to relate how thankful she was that both her girls survived, but how tragic it was that they both will live out their lives in chronic pain and with other serious disorders resulting from the accident.

As the evening came to a close, a MADD volunteer stood up and reminded the offenders that they were there to get a second chance—a second chance that people like Jan, Michele, Iris, and their families did not get. The 250 offenders then quietly filed out, many of them thanking the women, shaking their hands or hugging them. When one of the men reached Jan, he stopped and the two of them cried together. Later, tears still streaming down his face, that man said, "I'm so thankful I didn't cause this pain for someone else," and then promised that his second chance meant there wouldn't be a second offense.

The court decision forced these DUI offenders to go and hear what these victims had to say. But once they got there, they began to put themselves in another's shoes. They began to look at the reality of someone else's situation and to feel compassion. Hopefully, the next time that compassion will help them to do what is right—to not drive when drinking.

It was compassion that led Phyllis Chelsea to garner the strength to stop drinking—thus doing what was right for her children, her husband, and herself. She too had had alcoholic parents and had been accidentally lost by her mother, as her daughter had been. She knew what it felt like. And although it was good business for the H. B. Fuller secretary, Lorinda Tucker, to help her company's client, she no doubt also felt some compassion for the customer in his dilemma, which compelled her to go that extra mile. And for Tom and Pauline Nichter, it was compassion for the predicament of the stranger who had lost the gray folder that gave them the willpower to return what was not theirs.

When reviewing these examples, it becomes clear that compassion isn't unique to those with means. As William Bennett, former secretary of education, has said, "Compassion lies within the power of the mighty and the meek."

Compassion comes in all sizes and shapes. It is shown in both words and deeds. Compassion can be taking the time to listen to the troubles of a friend. It can be not hammering on the horn when a motorist is stalled in traffic or isn't ready to shoot across an intersection the second the light turns green. Compassion causes us to offer to baby-sit others' children when their parents really could use a break. It prompts us to volunteer at a library or a hospital, or simply to offer a seat to someone who looks tired. The number of opportunities that we have to demonstrate compassion is limited only by our will to act with integrity and caring.

As the MADD example illustrates, compassion can be taught. But the best way to foster compassion in others is to show compassion ourselves. Compassion isn't something that can be rudely demanded of others.

I believe that compassion most often results when we focus on our similarities. All of us, regardless of our background, experience love, sorrow, pain, pride, joy, and happiness. When we recognize this, we can be moved to compassion. It was this kind of compassion that moved Corrie Lynne and Gary Player to take home a two-month-old Eskimo baby and her two-and-a-half-year-old sister from the Alaska Children's Shelter in Anchorage. When the Players first saw the little girls, the wailing baby was strapped into an infant seat, and her sister sat defiantly beside her. Baby Sherri and Esmaralda Gay, or "Dolly," were abandoned children who needed foster parents.

The two children had been found on an Anchorage street corner and brought to the shelter by a state trooper. Dolly's teeth were rotten to the gums, and Sherri weighed a half pound less than she had when she was born. The girls were bruised, starved, and, in Dolly's case, the authorities sus-pected, sexually abused.

The process of helping Sherri and Dolly was long and trying, and it taught the Players some harsh lessons. One of the saddest was learning how to deal with the problem of an infant who was suffering withdrawal from alcohol addiction brought on by the mother's heavy and continual drinking throughout her pregnancy. The prescription boiled down to equal doses of compassion and patience, and plenty of both. The affected child will often shake and cry until hoarse, appearing to be completely inconsolable. Later in life, these children often suffer learning disorders that can be overcome only with long hours of individual attention. And more often than not, no matter how intense the efforts, the learning deficit is only partially overcome.

But the hardest part for Corrie and Gary was the heart-rending experience of watching helplessly as the legal system permitted the two children to be split up. When Sherri, the youngest, was taken to a new, potentially permanent home, the effect on Dolly was devastating. The Players considered it an act of God when, a few weeks later, the prospective adoptive parents returned Sherri because the baby hadn't stopped crying since the separation from her sister.

By this time, Corrie and Gary were falling deeply in love with the two children, and the children were also bonding with them. In the nurturing environment of the Players' home, the two children realized stability for the first time in their short lives. No one else—so it seemed—could handle Sherri and Dolly. But as much as the Players wanted to adopt the girls, the social services' policies were against allowing foster parents to adopt.

The Players tried everything to keep the girls, including

enlisting the cooperation of a local pediatrician, who promised to stall their medical records long enough for the Players to conjure up a workable strategy. It turned out to be unnecessary.

Within a year, the girls' biological mother had died of alcohol poisoning and the biological father, who had signed his rights away, disappeared. Immediately, the girls' status changed: the rules stated that they were now siblings without parents and had to be placed together. They were officially designated "hard to place," and thus were eligible for adoption by the Players, who immediately proceeded with the adoption of both girls.

As a direct outcome of the Players' compassion, Sherri and Dolly's lives were spared, and their future secured. After years of emotional support and counseling for the abuse she suffered, Dolly is now happily married, with four children of her own. And despite the serious learning disabilities brought on by fetal alcohol syndrome, Sherri eventually managed to do well, graduating from high school and attending college. She is now happily married with two children.

Earlier I stated that being fair means providing opportunities for others whenever possible and encouraging others to flourish, helping them to make the best use of their abilities. It is clear that Gary and Corrie Player went well beyond the call of duty that ordinary fairness requires, but it was compassion that led them to do it and to give the two girls opportunities that they might not otherwise have had. Compassion is the aspect of integrity that provides the strength and courage to fulfill such a demanding commitment.

But what is true compassion? Does it involve taking care

of others, or does it involve teaching others to become independent and to take care of themselves, as the Chelseas and the Players did? Traditionally it has been viewed as taking care of others. But at Amway, we believe that we show *greater* compassion when we help others care for themselves—helping them in a business context to achieve their full potential.

This doesn't mean that we never have to do things that cause pain for ourselves or others. The processes the Players and the Chelseas went through were riddled with pain for those involved. All of us probably know someone who has suffered the painful experience of losing a job, only to later attest that it was the best thing that ever happened, leading to greater happiness and fulfillment in some other kind of work.

We don't show compassion for others when we make excuses for them. Nor is compassion taking care of someone's needs forever if they are capable of caring for themselves. At Amway we have a number of employees who are physically or mentally challenged. We find them work that they are capable of doing and then hold them accountable. As a result, they hold their heads high and know the self-respect that comes from doing their jobs well and being self-reliant.

No matter what an individual's capability, reaching their full potential can be hindered if they are not encouraged to be self-reliant and personally responsible. There is nothing compassionate about making someone dependent on others.

True compassion flows solely from the hearts of individuals. Only then can it move out and be implemented through families, businesses, and communities. Properly guided, compassion can lead us to help others in such a way that they develop the personal freedom that comes from self-reliance. Thus, it propels us, not just from the head, but from the heart, to do what is right.

## 5

# Courage

Courage is the fifth component of integrity and is often associated with acts of heroism—such dramatic accounts as a motorist who rescues a mother and child from a burning automobile, or the teacher whose quick response to an emergency saves the life of a student. Undoubtedly, physical acts of heroism such as these are deserving of praise and attention. But it is not this kind of courage that I want to address. Rather, I want to discuss the courage we show in our day-to-day battles—that is, our moral courage: the courage to stand by our convictions. This is the kind of courage that springs from our strong belief in doing what is right rather than from a surge of adrenaline.

My father once said that life is not made up of a limited number of big decisions but a multitude of small ones. Our courage shows up every day in many small ways, but often demands risking some aspect of ourselves, whether it is our pride, our personal comfort, or even our livelihood. Moral courage gives us the strength to tell the truth at the risk of losing something, or to express an unpopular opinion at the risk of standing out in a crowd. Moral courage keeps us moving in one direction, without deviations caused by either fear or temptation. When we have courage, we can absorb difficulties and still continue to stride forward with poise and strength.

The Latin root of courage, *cor*, means "heart." We speak of the "heart of the matter" as the central or essential part of something. It would be appropriate to say, then, that moral courage is at the very heart of integrity, something we must have if we are going to be honest with others, or reliable and fair. Indeed, even the greatest acts of compassion require courage. Plato held courage in such high esteem that he classified it as one of the cardinal virtues.

Courage makes it possible to do what is right for the right reason. This actually is an important aspect of the Christian faith. Christians desire to do the right thing out of love and obedience to God and love for our neighbors, not because we are afraid of unpleasant consequences or because we may somehow benefit from it.

When we act with courage we gain integrity and the greater sense of inner freedom that comes with it. When we know we have done what is right, we live with a clear conscience. We are free of guilt and of the debilitating fear of getting caught. When we are honest with others, reliable, fair, and compassionate, we have no fear of being exposed as a liar or a cheat. This is not the courage to stand by our convictions as much as it is the courage that comes out of our convictions. And this kind of courage is a potent force indeed. Thomas Jefferson summed this up when he said, "One man of courage is a majority."

The deeper our convictions, the greater our ability to do what is right, and the more abundant and varied the opportunities to act with courage.

Meaningful acts of courage come in all shapes and sizes, and can be practiced by all of us. They include admitting our mistakes and imperfections, showing compassion for people to whom society has turned a blind eye, being accountable for ourselves and not trying to lay blame on others, acknowledging the good in others, resisting the temptation to lose our temper, putting our best foot forward, giving without getting, daring to reach for goals even if they seem to be outside our grasp, maintaining peace when the tendency is to fight, and fighting for what is right, especially when it is unpopular to do so.

Since having moral courage also lends us the strength to be honest about our emotions, then it should help us to laugh at the risk of appearing foolish, to cry at the risk of appearing sentimental, to state needs and expectations at the risk of being refused, to reach out to help others at the risk of becoming involved, to express hope at the risk of disappointment, and to love at the risk of not being loved in return.

Examples of moral courage are numerous. I have seen it in third-generation tobacco farmers who decided to plant corn instead of tobacco because they knew that smoking cigarettes is unhealthy and they could no longer be a part of that industry. And I've seen it in shareholders who turned down a lucrative offer because it would have resulted in the loss of jobs for thousands of employees.

A man in Greenwood, Indiana, had the courage to open a most unusual restaurant that reflected the principles and values he held dearest to his heart, despite many setbacks and warnings not to.

The kind of restaurant that Jonathan Byrd envisioned had so much variety that everyone who came, regardless of budget and individual tastes, could find something that they liked. He also wanted the convenience of a fast-food restaurant, where patrons could be seated immediately, where they could eat their meal without waiting on someone to serve them, and where customers could actually see what their meals would look like before ordering. If that wasn't a tall enough order, he wanted a family restaurant where patrons could feel comfortable praying together before they ate, where groups ranging in size from small scout troops to entire church organizations could come together and eat a hot meal under one roof, and most important to him, where alcohol was not on the menu. Byrd didn't have a restaurant to model his vision upon because to his knowledge none quite like it had ever existed.

Byrd's vision began to take shape when he was a young child and his father ran an ice-cream stand. By the time Byrd turned eleven, that ice-cream stand had expanded into the Kitchen Drive-In, just outside of Indianapolis, where Jonathan flipped burgers and made milk shakes. When he was fifteen his father became ill and Jonathan took on eighty-hour work weeks managing the restaurant and its sixty employees. He didn't mind the long hours because he loved everything about the restaurant business.

He developed an interest in cafeterias when, one Sunday, his parents started what became a family tradition of having lunch at a local cafeteria after church each week. He loved being able to pick up just what he wanted from the food on display. And even his younger sister, Janeen, a finicky eater, always found something she liked.

Another early experience that helped to shape Byrd's vision of his dream restaurant was when he and his pastor made a call on the grieving relatives of an entire family who had been instantly killed when their car was struck by a drunk driver. From that moment on Byrd was determined not to be part of any business that served or promoted liquor.

When Byrd enrolled at Cornell University's School of Hotel and Restaurant Management, he wrote his entrance paper on the relationship between the interstate highway system and cafeteria dining. Researching the paper helped Byrd to recognize the increasing need for fast-food preparation and delivery.

Byrd operated over twenty-five restaurants before he felt that he had the expertise and the money to turn his dreams into a reality. He sold his holdings in a chain of restaurants, opened a test kitchen to try out his recipes, and then went looking for a location where he could serve not only the local community but also many business travelers. He chose a property near one of America's major crossroads—in Greenwood, Indiana, just off Interstate 65 outside of Indianapolis—and started planning a restaurant that would be an entire acre under one roof, and would seat fourteen hundred people.

"Nearly twenty-five years had passed since I first started thinking about this restaurant," he said. "That's why my vision grew so large."

Everything that could go wrong did. The cost for permits

was ten times initial estimates. He spent tens of thousands of dollars more than anticipated by having to haul dirt to the site to bring it to the proper grade. After the concrete foundation was poured and the steel structure erected, a huge storm blew down all the roof trusses.

Byrd's contractor advised him to cut back on the quality of the building materials that he was using. Byrd wouldn't even entertain the notion. "I want this to be the kind of place that parents will be proud to bring their children," he told the contractor. "Mine included."

The most difficult day came when his pastor visited the construction site to relay a message from a fellow parishioner in the food distribution business. Because of the size of the restaurant Byrd was building, the selection of food he intended to offer, and the fact that he wasn't going to serve liquor—even at weddings and banquets—the parishioner expected Byrd to be bankrupt within six months.

Another visitor to the construction site that day was a businessman who said he planned to take over the structure for a giant funeral home when Byrd shut the doors to his restaurant, if indeed he ever got them open.

"I may have gotten a little depressed," Byrd admitted, "but my desire to build the restaurant never changed."

Each time he became fearful that all his efforts would be for nothing, he had only to remind himself of the vision that had guided him so far. He had the courage to pursue his dream because he believed in it.

Exactly seven months and seven days after breaking ground, the doors opened at Jonathan Byrd's Cafeteria and Banquet Hall. They have never closed. And in just over eight years of operation, the restaurant has served five million cus-

•

tomers. Prayers are routinely heard before meals begin. Gospel singers are on stage at least once a month. And alcohol is still not on the menu. Byrd's courage clearly paid off. Not only did it help him to do what he believed to be the right thing—it helped him realize his own dreams, thereby supporting his own personal freedom.

Another inspiring example of a person who had the courage to stick by her beliefs is that of a young nurse who felt compelled to do the right thing, despite the fact that it put her career and livelihood at stake. For reasons that will become apparent, she has asked that her real name not be used in this book, so I will call her Katherine.

Katherine's story begins in a large Kentucky hospital where she worked as a registered nurse in the cancer ward. It was 5 A.M. on a Saturday, and she was one of four nurses assigned to cover the east wing of the fourth floor. Her tasks included giving medications, taking temperatures, and handling patient emergencies.

A call came for Katherine to tend to an eighty-three-year-old leukemia patient who was undergoing chemotherapy treatment. When Katherine got to the room, the patient's son was standing over his father's bed. The son had rung the call bell. By accident, his father had pulled out the intravenous tubing that was used to administer the potent chemotherapy drug.

Because the patient was asleep, Katherine didn't want to turn on the overhead light. She merely set about reconnecting the IV as she had done hundreds of times before. After clearing the catheter through which the chemotherapy drug passed, Katherine reached for the bag containing the patient's extra tubing and flushing solution. There she found a pale blue bottle with a white label. In the dim light she could just make out the word "chloride." Certain that this was the drug she was looking for, she drew off 5 cc into a syringe and injected the liquid into the tubing.

No sooner had she administered the drug than the patient suddenly sat bolt upright in bed, clutching at his heart. Katherine pulled back on the syringe and dropped the bottle. Her patient convulsed in agony, then slumped back in the bed. Katherine immediately signaled for the hospital's special emergency life-support team.

Within minutes a doctor and a team of nurses were bent over the patient, frantically trying to revive him. Electric paddles were applied to his chest. The shock was just enough to jolt the patient's heart back to life, but he was left in a coma, from which he would never recover.

"What did you give him?" the doctor asked.

Katherine told him "Sodium chloride," and the doctor came to the logical conclusion that a blood clot must have dislodged from the catheter and gotten caught in the man's heart. Katherine was not blamed for any wrongdoing and was sent back to her station.

Despite the doctor's conclusion, Katherine worried that somehow she was responsible for what had happened. So later that night she returned to the patient's room and retrieved the blue bottle she had dropped during the seizure. Looking at the bottle in the light, she now could see the mistake she had made. The bottle was not marked "sodium chloride" after all. It read "potassium chloride," a highly concentrated form of potassium. To Katherine's knowledge, this powerful drug had no reason even to be in the room, let alone in the bag containing her patient's flushing solution.

Now she was faced with an agonizing dilemma. Reporting

the accident could mean getting fired and potentially losing her nursing license. There was also a good chance that the patient's family would sue the hospital. If she did not report the accident, the hospital records would state that the heart attack was caused by a blood clot dislodged from the catheter, and she would keep her job.

Katherine also thought about the patient. No matter what happened, he had only a short time to live, and did, in fact, die three days later. Her coming forward could do nothing to change his condition.

Katherine left the hospital that night still struggling with her dilemma. As much as she wanted to come forward and tell the truth, she kept thinking of her son and daughter. Since the children's father had left them two years earlier, Katherine had barely managed to make ends meet. She was constantly behind on paying the bills and had been doing double shifts at the hospital trying to catch up. She couldn't imagine how she was going to provide for her children if she lost her job. At the same time, she didn't want to live a lie.

By the time she returned for her next shift she had decided to tell her story to a superior, who, in turn, advised her to keep it to herself. It was, after all, an honest mistake, and the man was old and very ill and would die soon anyway. But Katherine chose not to take that advice, so she went a level higher. The hospital administrators felt they had no choice but to suspend Katherine immediately. And three days later she was fired. Pending a hearing by the State Board of Nursing, there was a chance that she would be prevented from ever working as a nurse again.

Though devastated by the experience, Katherine knew

she had done the right thing. "I could get up in the morning and look at myself in the mirror," she said.

Katherine counted on and received the support of her church. A friend hired her as a receptionist. She then took a job as an office temp, and her income went from $25,000 to $7,000. She sold almost all of her furniture, and her children went without new shoes and ate plenty of peanut-butter-and-jelly sandwiches.

Eight months after the accident, the State Board of Nursing decided to put her on a two-year probation rather than take away her license. When the two years were up, she wasn't permitted to return to the hospital that had fired her, but she eventually found a better position at another hospital.

Katherine says that not once did she regret the decision she made. Just the opposite. As news of what she had done reached friends and associates, she was flooded with calls. Among the callers were doctors and other nurses, who, like herself, had accidentally killed a patient. Unlike her, they never reported their mistakes, and were paying a price for it.

As this story well illustrates, acting with integrity and the courage of our convictions not only guides us in upholding the freedom and rights of others, it also sets *us* free. As Katherine says of those who called her: "They had become slaves of their own guilt—prisoners of their own conscience. The truth had set me free."

The reason Katherine took her truthful course of action can be found in the depth of her conviction. It is impossible to act courageously about something if we don't feel it is important. Katherine valued integrity over her own short-term self-interest. This is what gave her the courage to come forward, provided her the strength to carry on, and ultimately put her life back together.

If citizens today appear less courageous than in previous generations, perhaps it is the weakness of their beliefs that is at the root of the problem. If Pauline and Tom Nichter had not held a deep belief in the importance of honesty, they would not have had the willpower to turn over the money they had found to the police. If Phyllis and Andy Chelsea did not have an overwhelming respect for the humanity of their community, they wouldn't have had the strength to fight so hard to breathe life into it. And if Corrie Lynne and Gary Player had not felt such deep compassion for the two little girls they took in, God only knows where those girls would be now.

I believe that my courage comes from my faith in God. I cannot imagine courage without faith. I don't always know what God's plan is, but my faith helps me to hold steadfast no matter what circumstances confront me.

It requires courage to do the right thing: to speak the truth when it is not popular; to discipline our children when it is easier just to ignore their inappropriate behavior; or to get involved in public debate, whether in our schools, our communities, or on a state or national level. Armchair quarterbacking does not take courage. But it does take courage and faith to do what is right, not when we *know* what the end results are going to be, but when the results are not clear. We must speak out *before* the vote is counted. As my friend Rabbi Lapin so aptly puts it, "All of human greatness is *precisely* acting before all the data is in."

A little plaque that sits on my father's desk says, "It's not the size of the man in the fight, but the size of the fight in the man." As this saying illustrates, our capacity for courage is not determined by physical strength, age, or gender, but by the strength of our convictions and the readiness to act upon them. For this reason it is crucial that we understand the importance and purpose of the values that we hold, and that we have the courage to defend them and pass them on to others.

Courage, the heart of integrity, gives us the strength to be honest, reliable, fair, and to act on our compassion. And as these stories illustrate, it also gives us a personal freedom. Indeed, courage, like compassion, is integral to maintaining our freedom and doing what is right. It takes courage to do what is right because often it means we face adversity by not accepting the status quo.

# 6

# Humility

As with compassion and courage, humility is integral to our personal integrity and to preserving freedom. Humbling ourselves is part of doing what is right and helps us be more aware of others' concerns. It promotes honesty with ourselves and about ourselves. It is aligning ourselves with the truth. Oftentimes finding humility requires a process of self-examination, which may occur behind closed doors or in concert with others to whom we are accountable. It isn't always an easy process. We must force ourselves to look closely in the mirror.

Humility is necessary if we are to be honest, reliable, or fair with others. Humility requires doing what is right before succumbing to our own personal desires. It means not being boastful or prideful and promoting ourselves at the expense of others. Humility calls on us to accept the fact that we are all created equal.

My father-in-law, Ed Prince, was a man of true humility. While I always knew this, it became even more evident to me after his death. I can't count the people who came up to Betsy and me at her father's funeral service and told us stories of Ed's generosity and kindness, always done quietly, without fanfare, and with humility. His generosity, charity, and philanthropy were boundless, yet nearly all were carried out anonymously. Ed never wanted to call attention to what he believed was only what God had called him to do.

One man told us of the time he moved down to Holland from Michigan's Upper Peninsula to work for the Prince Corporation. At the time, the real estate situation in the Upper Peninsula was grim, and the man had been unable to sell his home there. He became strapped financially, with payments and taxes on two homes. Somehow, Ed learned about the man's predicament and bought the property in the Upper Peninsula, holding on to it himself until it sold. No one except this man ever knew about Ed's good deed.

Shortly after my father-in-law's death, I was trying to reach a man who had been a key advisor to Betsy's parents and to the company. Not knowing his number, I checked with directory assistance, but the man who answered was the wrong person. He mentioned that he had received many "wrong number" calls for this person—and then went on to tell me his own "Ed Prince" story. When he and several others were trying to raise funds to buy and equip a van for a paraplegic friend, this man had contacted Ed, knowing him as a local business owner who might have the resources to help. The two men had never met, but Ed generously gave the financial aid they needed.

I could go on and on, recounting examples of the gracious, humble spirit of this man, but let one more suffice. Each year, Junior Achievement of West Michigan recognizes several outstanding citizens with their "Business Hall of Fame" awards. In late 1994, they told Ed that they would like him to be a recipient of the award in the coming year. Ed's immediate reaction was to decline the honor. He had always shunned public awards and recognition, not wishing to draw attention to himself. Betsy finally convinced her father to accept the award, but she ended up accepting it for him. By that time, Ed had already gone to his greater reward.

It's unfortunate that humility is frequently characterized as evidence of low self-esteem, self-pity, or timidity. Nothing could be further from the truth. Humility is not a weakness but a strength. And pride, its opposite, causes much more difficulty than humility ever could. As one proverb nicely describes it, "Pride goes before destruction, a haughty spirit before a fall."

Perhaps the most misunderstood aspect of humility is that of submission. A person of humility recognizes that there is a greater reality and that there are more profound principles to which we must submit ourselves. Submission to the principles of integrity, for instance, allows us to properly honor and uphold the freedom and rights of others in a consistent fashion.

Humility comes out of the recognition that an individual's life is but one part of a whole, a whole that I see as a master plan. We are not islands, nor are we laws unto ourselves.

I personally find it a lot easier to be humble when I recognize that I am the created, not the Creator, and that I am, as a human being, essentially disobedient to God. I believe that we lose our sense of humility when we begin to imagine ourselves as better than others. As a Christian, I acknowledge that what I have—whether loved ones, a talent or a gift, or property—are gifts from God. As quickly as they are given, they can be taken away. For me, submission to our Creator is fundamental to breaking down the tendency toward self-centeredness and the misguided sense of self-importance we humans so often struggle with. We are the *vehicles* for good rather than the source of good in our lives.

My belief that everyone is created by God also makes it easier for me to honor the freedom and rights of others. This belief does not diminish me; it simply raises everyone around me. It also helps me to acknowledge the specialness of others and leaves no ground for conceit.

Humility helps us to acknowledge that we do not have control over our environment or the circumstances of our birth: our innate talents and gifts, our physical bodies, or our parent's financial situation. Humility helps us face these circumstances with grace and also helps us to make good choices in reacting to them. And how we choose to react to our circumstances—I believe—has more impact on our future than the circumstances themselves.

Humility gives us the confidence to accept and to admit our own mistakes, to apologize, to listen, to feel gratitude for the good in our lives, and to forgive ourselves and those around us for mistakes they, and we, inevitably make. It keeps us flexible in our opinions and brings about a willingness to see the good and even the potential greatness in others. Humility is the foundation of respect, for it permits us to cultivate friendship by supporting without flattering, giving feedback without offending, and encouraging without being condescending. Humility can also bring about generosity, kind acceptance, and tolerance. It is quick to give credit or assume responsibility where it is warranted. And it is unselfish and free from arrogance or ostentation. Humble people are honest about their own strengths and accomplishments and don't require external validation to prop themselves up.

When we are honest about our imperfections, as well as our talents and abilities, we are better able to identify where to apply our hard work and efforts—both to hone those talents and to improve upon the weak areas. We can be better relied upon to roll up our sleeves and work hard—to be the best we can be and to do the best we can do, wherever we find ourselves, whether it be in the back kitchen of a restaurant, on the battleground, or in the boardroom.

A man well known for his humility and for doing his best is Gus Pagonis, a retired general, and an executive vice president at Sears Roebuck. You may remember him as the officer who earned his third star for directing the movement and supply of U.S. troops during Operation Desert Storm, which has been recognized as the greatest logistical feat in modern military history.

Pagonis says that he learned the meaning of humility while working at his father's restaurant, the Pagonis, a twenty-four-hour, seven-day-a-week restaurant in Charleroi, Pennsylvania. The Pagonis was the kind of restaurant where everyone in the family had to pitch in to keep it operating smoothly. So the first job Gus had there was as a shoeshine boy. This was the same job his father had when he first emigrated from Greece. The elder Pagonis had particular ideas as to how the customer was supposed to be treated. By the time Gus was ten years old he had graduated to cleaning tables and working as the janitor. Again, his father, who had once done the job himself, had exacting standards that he expected to be met.

"You can never be too humble to do a good job," his father always said. "Don't be afraid to get your hands dirty, no matter what your status."

Pagonis met his father's exacting standard. No matter how menial the task, he did it well. This was true even when Pagonis returned home to the family restaurant after having been away in the army for two years and having just been promoted to captain. Pagonis remembers, "I was full of pride and eager to show off my uniform. But the first thing Dad says is that it's the janitor's day off and couldn't I clean the bathrooms that night." After a moment's hesitation, Pagonis changed out of his uniform and put on an apron. His choice that night became a pivotal moment in his life, for to a great extent, he has been wearing that apron ever since. In Pagonis, fellow soldiers found a man who didn't let status, rank, or an inflated ego stand in the way of getting the job done and doing it right.

Humility prevents arrogance or self-importance. It's quite appropriate that the young Pagonis didn't mind getting his hands dirty, since the word "humility" comes out of the Latin *humus,* or "soil." Humility suggests that our feet are flat on the ground—that we have a down-to-earth common sense about ourselves. People with humility can acknowledge their strengths and abilities and can receive praise and support without it going to their head. Similarly, they can defer to greater experience than their own without losing self-confidence. But there is another quality of humility that can't be ignored: a genuine respect for and desire to serve others. Thus humility is an essential element of upholding others' freedom, and doing what is right. I like to think of it as the rich soil out of which much greatness springs.

A great and brilliant man who spent a lifetime practicing humility was the late Harold Edgerton, the scientist who pioneered stop-action and high-speed photography. He is best remembered as the man who made time stand still with his photographs of a droplet of milk as it splashed into a saucer, and of the fanlike image made by a gold club as a golfer swung to drive a ball. His technological achievements helped to safeguard American troops landing in Normandy and made possible the tracking of hummingbird movements by animal behaviorists. His forty-plus patented inventions are found on cameras, skyscrapers, airport runways, submarines, photocopiers, and automobile engines.

As a result of his inventions, Edgerton became a millionaire many times over. He could easily have lived a life of leisure, or simply indulged himself in his personal scientific interests within the cloisters of the Massachusetts Institute of Technology, his alma mater. Yet he remained, first and foremost, a teacher and a servant of others, whether it was helping an English oceanographer find a sunken ship, or showing a foreign exchange student the way back to his dorm.

Born in Freemont, Nebraska, Edgerton paid his way through the University of Nebraska by working as an electrician, a lineman, a coal handler, and a movie projectionist. This made him very "handy to have around the house," his sister, Mary Ellen Pogue, remembers. He could fix practically anything, and took immense joy in using his gifts to help others. He lived a plain, simple life guided by the fundamental values he learned at the First Christian Church he attended. He never smoked, rarely drank, and seldom uttered an oath stronger than "heck."

While attending MIT as a graduate student, the twenty-four-year-old Edgerton began the experiment that set the course for the rest of his life. He needed to get a look at the rotors of a spinning electric motor he was studying. But the only way to do that, he reasoned, was with a series of brief but powerful bursts of light that were synchronized with the speed of the motor. This seemed like a simple enough task, except that the kind of equipment he needed wasn't commercially available. Conventional flashbulbs and incandescent lights didn't work, so Edgerton decided to build an intensely bright "strobe" light. It took him a day to build the first one. He then spent the rest of his career perfecting it.

This single discovery began a lifetime position on the MIT faculty and a highly successful career in business. Edgerton teamed up with colleagues to start an engineering company they called EG&G—a company that grew to be worth $2 billion, and to employ twenty-three thousand people in the United States and in sixteen foreign countries. Among its products were airport runway lights and instruments that read the DNA of cells.

With characteristic humility Edgerton looked back to the day he built his first strobe light, crediting a colleague for making the observation that triggered the creative process that has affected all of our lives, in one way or another.

"Why don't you do something useful with the light instead of fooling around with motors?" his colleague asked.

"What could I do with a flashing light?" Edgerton asked.

"The whole world is moving," was the reply.

And indeed it was. Like the moving parts on the motor he was studying, there were literally thousands of things that were moving too quickly for the human eye to see. With this in mind Edgerton proceeded to design photographic systems that would capture a bullet leaving the barrel of a gun, a balloon exploding, and a cat's tongue lapping milk, and thus was born modern high-speed flash photography.

Despite the fact that his photographs have become classics of science as well as modern art exhibited at the Museum of Modern Art, he remained humble about his accomplishments. "Don't make me out as an artist," he said. "I'm only an engineer."

This, of course, is true enough. Yet it is also true that Edgerton shot hundreds of photographs of his classic milk drop before he got the one in which the crown points of the splash were just right.

Edgerton enjoyed handing out his photographs as much as he relished tackling assignments for anyone who asked for his aid. Off North Carolina's Cape Hatteras he helped fellow scientists pinpoint and recover the *Monitor*, the sunken Civil War naval vessel. He explored the ocean floor with Jacques Cousteau and the crew of the *Calypso*, who nicknamed him "Papa Flash." He developed a sonar system, which he used to sound St. Mark's Canal in Venice for the legendary lost column of Luxor. He also helped search for Scotland's Loch Ness monster.

His true love, however, was teaching. He loved nothing more than sharing his knowledge and helping others to take it further. His open houses were a popular ritual for three generations of students, as were his evening sing-alongs during which he played the guitar. Often, at these get-togethers,

Edgerton's discussions with his students changed their lives when he helped them to see the potential good that could come out of their own work. To these students he was a cheerleader and sometimes a partner. More often than not, his partnerships were sealed with only a handshake.

Nowhere was Edgerton's humility more apparent than in the classroom. One of his students describes an occasion when he eagerly presented an idea to Edgerton, who congratulated and encouraged the student, saying, "That's a fine idea." Only later did the student learn that Edgerton had originated the concept years earlier.

When times were tough, Edgerton saw to it that bright and devoted students and colleagues had jobs, even if it meant that he was the one who was paying their salaries. Often these people didn't know he was their benefactor. When one of his students complained that he couldn't get a car loan, Edgerton offered to sign for him. The salesman reportedly took one look at Edgerton's rumpled suit, run-down shoes, his watch with its broken crystal, and hesitated. But a call to Edgerton's bank quickly settled the matter.

"He was worth millions," a former student and later dean of MIT has said, "but took pleasure in never showing it—that is, until it came time to endow an electrical engineering building or a scholarship fund for needy students."

Edgerton was known for his boundless energy and enthusiasm for life. His love of learning played no small part in this. "I came here to learn," he told colleagues after his fortieth anniversary as an MIT professor. "And I'm still learning."

One could argue that Edgerton—as did the Players in adopting Dolly and Sherri—went well beyond the call of duty when it came to being fair, to providing opportunities for others whenever possible and respecting others' rights to flourish and to make the best possible use of their abilities. But he would probably argue that "to whom much is given, much is expected." Certainly Edgerton met any and all expectations—and his humility had much to do with that.

Perhaps the most notable outcome of humility, as Edgerton's brilliant career demonstrates, is that it compels us to expand our horizons by gaining greater knowledge and skill. The mechanics of this are simple. A willingness to recognize the great and valuable knowledge accumulated by those who have gone before opens us to learning from them. And when we can acknowledge that we do not have all the answers, learning becomes a natural process.

The more we learn, and the more genuine information we acquire, the more honest, reliable, and fair we can be—and the better decisions we can make for ourselves. Thus, humility not only leads to greater integrity and the ability to uphold the freedom of others; it, like courage, also provides us with more personal freedom.

# 7

# Reason

R eason is the component of integrity that is essential to the thought process. If we do not think about what we do, our actions are impulsive. They are not the actions of a person with integrity.

Reason prevents courage from becoming recklessness, and compassion from fostering dependence.

Reasoning lends greatly to our ability to do what is right, because to "do what is right," we have to *know* what is right. To practice honesty we must be able to discern how to tell the truth in a way that is truly honest. Being reliable, which requires rationality, also calls on the thought process—as does fairness, which requires judgment and prudence.

Similarly, reason helps us to distinguish between misguided compassion and compassion that is really helpful—and, as previously noted, it prevents courage from becoming recklessness. Humility, which involves the recognition and acceptance that some things are beyond our control, also benefits from the ability to think things through. A popular prayer, attributed to Saint Francis of Assisi, captures the role of reasoning in this regard: "God, give me the serenity to accept what cannot be changed, the courage to change what should be changed, and the wisdom to distinguish one from the other."

While I cannot claim that thinking things through will guarantee wisdom, it is safe to say that we will not achieve wisdom without doing so. Nor can I claim that our ability to reason and to discern right from wrong can ever be flawless. In fact, I believe, in accordance with my faith, that man's nature is fundamentally imperfect, and therefore requires grounding in the eternal wisdom from above. But as the Proverbs instruct, "Wisdom is the principal thing; therefore get wisdom. And in all your getting, get understanding . . . and when you walk, your steps will not be hindered, and when you run, you will not stumble." God gives us wisdom, intelligence, and the ability to reason.

The process of reasoning not only supports our integrity, but, like courage and humility, it also provides us with personal freedom in a more direct way. Many of our great philosophers have suggested that the human ability to think and to reason is what truly allows us to be free. As Aristotle pointed out, if one lacks reason, then one lacks choice, and therefore, one lacks freedom. When we use our ability to think, we are put into a position to make choices and thereby uphold the freedom that we have.

To realize the importance of reason, one only has to imagine life without it. A good many problems that occur today are less a result of bad intentions, and more a result of a refusal to think. Frequently mistakes, hurt feelings, breakdowns in communication, fender benders, and deadly accidents happen because someone is "asleep at the wheel," either literally or metaphorically. In other words, one is not fully conscious of what one is doing or saying or of the subsequent consequences.

The late Herman Kahn, a renowned mathematician, physicist, economist, and futurist, was a man who believed that we should attempt to think through and gain understanding of everything that we can and that nothing should be ignored or overlooked when planning for the future. His guiding belief was that rational analysis is critical. His "reasoning" helped to shape policy making through eight presidential administrations.

Kahn made it his business to analyze, probe, and question the consequences of military and other policy decisions that would determine our nation's future. He was a man who didn't like being surprised or victimized by events. He believed that people need thinking tools as well as facts to help cope with history before it happens.

To those who knew him, Kahn seemed every bit the absentminded professor. He was an immense man, described as both brooding and sparkling, eclectic and intense. With an IQ of 200, he had an intellect that impressed everyone he met. Even as a child his prodigious talents were obvious to anyone who knew him. He had a photographic memory, and equally important, he could quickly extract and distill the essence of books or lectures. He also had a form of mental "peripheral vision" that made it possible for him to do two or three things at the same time. He could be writing a paper on nuclear physics and at the same time play a game of bridge and watch a basketball game on television. An incredulous high-school teacher is reputed to have once caught Kahn reading a science-fiction magazine during class, only to discover that he could recite, word for word, the lecture the teacher had been giving.

There have been, however, other intellects as brilliant as Kahn's. What distinguished Kahn was his commitment to thinking things through, no matter how unpleasant the topic or the possible conclusions.

Kahn began his work at UCLA, and then moved to Cal Tech, but it wasn't until he joined the Rand Corporation and later formed his own think tank, the Hudson Institute, that he truly drew public attention. His first groundbreaking and controversial book, *On Thermonuclear War*, which he followed with *Thinking About the Unthinkable*, popularized the vocabulary of "first strikes," "escalation," and "megatons." These books set off a firestorm of controversy because they confronted a subject that the general public wasn't prepared to contemplate. He argued that not "thinking" objectively about something as "unthinkable" as nuclear war only made the threat of nuclear war more probable. Since it was impossible to "disinvent" the existence of nuclear weapons, it was vital to understand their full implications.

"Shooting the messenger," he liked to say, "is the wrong way to deal with bad news."

Kahn's interest went far beyond the threat of nuclear war. He studied economic trends and predicted, for example, Japan's great economic boom well before Japanese cars began flooding our market.

Although few of us are gifted with anything approaching

Kahn's great mental capacity, his example is something we all can learn from. Kahn made his mind an open door. He was continually reasoning things through and seeking feedback, from national leaders and taxi drivers alike. This approach permitted him to consider the "unthinkable"—not only for himself, but for the rest of us.

As Kahn would emphasize, an important outcome of thinking things through is that we are better able to learn from our own and others' mistakes, to make a direct connection between probable cause and effect, and to discern the true consequences of the choices we have to make *before* we make them. Through reasoning, we become better stewards of our own freedom and are more equipped to uphold the freedom of others—to do what is right.

Judge Charles McClure, who presides over juvenile court in Leon County, Florida, is someone who effectively teaches young offenders the consequences of their choices by forcing them to think about them. In an era of moral ambivalence in the judicial system, he has a "unique" perspective on his responsibilities as a judge: He believes that the punishment should fit the crime.

In McClure's court, a young man who claimed he had no money to pay restitution for damage he had done was forced to hand his wristwatch over to the courts. A youth who vandalized school property was ordered to repair that same property. Other sentences included emptying trash cans at the local landfill, caring for abused dogs and cats at an animal shelter, and organizing a crime-prevention program at a local school. Convicted juvenile offenders in McClure's court also have their pictures printed in the newspapers. And in one case, the offender's parents, who apparently had not provided adequate supervision of their child, were forced to serve a sentence along with their child. McClure has also taken the unique step of drafting legislation that would require parents to sign promissory notes endorsing restitution to victims.

"These sentences are not symbolic gestures," one of McClure's fans says. "They're designed to give young people something to think about, to elicit responsible behavior."

McClure's commonsense approach to sentencing is a result of the years he spent in traffic court watching children get bailed out of trouble. He got so tired of a system that sent the wrong message to the offender that he instituted a program in which juvenile offenders who had been caught driving dangerously had to work on Friday and Saturday nights opening and closing doors in the emergency room of the local hospital. All participants subsequently had to answer detailed questions about what they had observed so that McClure knew they had taken the time to reflect upon the potential consequences of their behavior.

One of the first offenders he put in that program is now a respected Tallahassee attorney. "The young man saw the body of a friend being wheeled into the emergency room after a motorcycle accident," McClure says. "That experience made more of an impression on him than any sentence I could have given him."

Judge McClure is mindful of the fact that the pace of modern life, filled with incessant stimuli, oftentimes makes it difficult to find time to think—or, as some put it, to "hear ourselves think." This is why he often requires that young people write term papers and reports about their behavior and the potential consequences.

The pace of life is such that we often feel we are on a treadmill. The daily routine for many of us consists of racing from home to work, or from home to school, then to lessons or practice, to the supermarket, and then back home to cook and keep house. It often seems implausible to stop and take the time to reflect on the challenges of life. And then too frequently the precious time we do have is spent in front of the television set.

According to Home Together, a San Diego organization that encourages reduced TV watching, by the time the average child graduates from high school, he or she will have spent fifteen thousand hours in front of the television set, as compared to eleven thousand hours in the classroom. And by the time the average American reaches the age of sixty-five, he or she will have spent a total of nine years in front of the television. Watching television can lull us into not thinking independently, and it makes us lazy—simply because something is reported on TV we tend to believe that it must be true. Apparently, we not only believe that the news reports must be true but that the entertainment programs are true as well. According to Home Together, two hundred thousand people wrote to Marcus Welby, M.D., seeking medical advice! Meanwhile, we are getting our news and other information in six-second sound bites.

While we can't possibly become expert at everything, we need to seek out ideas and opinions from people we trust—the news makers rather than the news reporters. We must actively seek out good information and we must not get lazy and let others do it for us. The Apostle John recorded Jesus as saying, "You shall know the truth and the truth shall set you free." Taking the responsibility of knowing the facts about the world we live in and accepting the truth of our creation provides the moral compass we need to navigate often murky waters and frees us to live as we should.

While we must find ways of getting quality information, we must also find ways to stimulate our own creative thought processes. Instead of sitting in front of the television, consider how beneficial it would be to have thoughtful conversations with family and friends about current issues and concerns that are on our minds, and to read more about critical matters of our times. It is equally important to find ways to carve out time for quiet reflection. We can set aside a few minutes each day to think about decisions we have to make—getting up a few minutes earlier, turning the car radio off for a while, or pausing for a moment at the end of each day to consider the day's challenges or tomorrow's plans. I also take time out of my day to seek guidance through prayer. This, together with some quiet reflection, has gotten me through some challenging times.

If we wish to maintain our freedom, we are going to have to wake up and think things through. Reasoning is not only essential to the process of doing what is right, it is also a key to personal freedom.

## 8

# Self-discipline

Self-discipline, the last component of integrity, is crucial to our ability to do what is right. Without it, we could hardly resist life's temptations to lie, cheat, take credit where it isn't due, or break a promise. Self-discipline helps us to remain strong in the face of any temptation to impose on the freedom and rights of others in favor of our own self-interest.

Also, like courage, humility, and thoughtfulness, self-discipline directly supports our personal freedom. This is where the self in self-discipline comes in. To be ruled by our passions ignores prudence and the courage to do what is right.

Self-discipline is rooted in action rather than quiet contemplation. It is proactive. It involves trading today's pleasures for tomorrow's benefits, and means not only taking control of our appetites, but taking control of all that we do, whether it is keeping to a budget, maintaining a pleasant disposition, or (in my case) being punctual.

I'm often asked why I choose to work ten or twelve hours each day given the fact that my family's net worth is such that I don't really have to work. My response is "to whom much is given, much is expected and required." But it takes a good dose of self-discipline to do what is expected and required when one's food and shelter are not dependent upon it.

My siblings and I lived a fairly normal middle-class childhood, since at that time Amway was small and in the early stages of growth. Today, however, our own children and nieces and nephews are growing up in an environment where all of their needs and wants could be met. Their opportunities are great, but that also includes even greater opportunities to make bad decisions. While our children can rely on the discipline Betsy and I provide as parents, when they reach adulthood, only their own values, principles, and self-discipline will keep them on the right track.

Our friend Neal Plantinga, author and theologian, says that self-discipline is "no rival to freedom; it is, in fact, freedom's very base and possibility." We cannot be free without it. And the fewer external restraints one has, the more internal controls are required if one is to be truly free.

When we waste our time, resources, and talents in pursuit of pleasure, self-indulgence, or self-aggrandizement, we do not gain freedom. We lose it! We become dependent on others to provide our pleasure, to make our decisions, to boost our ego, and even to take care of us. We become slaves to our basest drives and passions.

Mahatma Gandhi held self-restraint to be the third cardinal principle, without which the first two principles, truth and nonviolence, could hardly be put into effect. While there are many benefits to be had by disciplining ourselves for more practical reasons, it also serves higher purposes. For example, a Christian must use reason and conscience to *know* God's will; but self-discipline is essential in order to *do* God's will.

Through self-discipline we are able to form good habits so that a conscious act of will is not required for every small decision we must make. Self-discipline is a way of building automatic responses so that when temptation comes along, it doesn't overpower us. The boxing champion Joe Frazier described this response when he talked about going into a fight. "It all comes down to conditioning and reflexes," Frazier said. "Because when things aren't going the way you planned, that's often all you've got. If you cheated in the dark of the morning, you'll be found out under the bright lights in the stadium."

Unfortunately, many people today confuse self-discipline with rigidity or inflexibility. This is not what is meant by self-discipline. Self-discipline is making the right choices based on our moral compass and not being bumped off course by our temptations. It's having the self-control to set priorities for ourselves and to make choices between conflicting desires in a clear-sighted and evenhanded manner.

Self-discipline combined with prudence breeds integrity. It also fosters the patience to accept delays, difficulties, and disappointments with peace and understanding and without anger, discouragement, or despair. This combination also keeps us steadfast, helping us to persevere in difficult circumstances.

Self-discipline combined with reason brings about good manners and civility, even when we would rather tell someone they should be "hung out to dry." Most importantly, self-discipline allows us to act with integrity—resulting in consistently telling the truth, keeping our promises, and acting in a fair manner. A person without self-discipline cannot be trusted to do what is right, especially when the going gets tough.

Many people have demonstrated self-discipline in outstanding ways, but one example in particular comes to mind. Colin Powell, the former chairman of the Joint Chiefs of Staff, has made self-discipline a way of life. His philosophy is a simple one: Mastery of the little things in life is a means of tackling the bigger things.

Powell grew up in New York, the son of immigrants from Jamaica. Powell's father, Luther, was a shipping clerk in the garment district. His mother, Maude, was a seamstress. They lived in one of the toughest neighborhoods in the Bronx, where drugs and crime were constant temptations for young people. For Powell, self-discipline was not only the key to survival, it was the ticket to a better life.

Hard work was expected of the Powell children, and Colin was eager to comply. At the age of seventeen, he took a job at a soft-drink bottling plant, where he earned ninety cents an hour. Although he would have preferred manning one of the bottling machines, his job was to mop the floors.

That summer Powell mopped what seemed like acres of sticky cola-stained floors. Instead of complaining, he strove to be the best mop handler who had ever worked in the bottling business. When he was tempted to complain that other workers were getting promotions over him, he consciously focused his thoughts on the task at hand and just kept mopping. One day, he thought it was more than he could bear when fifty cases of cola came crashing to the cement and he was assigned to clean up the mess. But his self-discipline paid off. Powell's employer came to trust and respect his diligence and reliability, and the next summer, he was promoted to a job loading bottles onto the filling machine. The summer after that he was made deputy foreman.

What happened after that is well known. Powell joined an ROTC training program at City College of New York, served in Vietnam, and then attended graduate school at George Washington University. Over the next several years, Powell went on to distinguish himself in a series of assignments in the military. His self-discipline and hard work eventually landed him the position of National Security Advisor for President Ronald Reagan. It was during this two-year assignment that he caught the attention of the then Vice President Bush, who later appointed Powell chairman of the Joint Chiefs of Staff. Powell was not only the first member of a minority to hold this position, he was also the youngest person ever to do so.

His rise to prominence, as extraordinary as it may seem, didn't come as a surprise to people who had worked with him, including those who watched him mop the cement floors at the bottling plant. This was a young man who planned to succeed through self-discipline and hard work. His self-discipline led him to positions of great responsibility because others believed they could trust him to consistently do the right thing, even under great pressure.

There is no doubt that it took self-discipline for Tom and Pauline Nichter to turn in the gray folder they found, despite their serious need for money. It took self-discipline for Cal Ripken to consistently show up and do his best, year after year; for Robert George of Medallion Construction to resist taking advantage of his subcontractor's mistake; and for Katherine the nurse to live her life consistent with the truth.

Self-discipline is required for us to maintain our integrity and to be relied upon to always do what is right, even when we seem to have every reason not to. Self-discipline also helps facilitate accomplishment.

How many times did Thomas Edison try and fail in his attempts to perfect the lightbulb? Perseverance played an important role in this process, and perseverance requires self-discipline. There are many highly accomplished and talented people in the world, but they didn't just wake up one day to find themselves successful. Accomplishments, whether they are musical, athletic, or commercial, are a result of hours and hours of work, training, or practicing—hours invested through self-discipline.

The necessity for self-discipline is also recognized by one of Colin Powell's longtime friends, John Henry Stanford. A retired army general, Stanford made up his mind to take on what he considers the greatest challenge facing the United States today: to bring self-discipline to a generation of children brought up to believe that "good" means "easy."

After his distinguished career in the military, and then a term as Fulton County executive, in Atlanta, Georgia, Stanford had a myriad of options available to him. A man of his organizational talents would have been welcomed in the private sector, and rewarded handsomely. He could have run for political office, or he could have retired. Instead, he took on a task he calls his "next great adventure." His "adventure" entailed bringing leadership to one of the largest school systems in the country, where the dropout rate was fifteen percent, and nearly one-third of the parents with school-age children in the district placed their children in private schools.

The first thing that is unusual about Seattle's newest

school superintendent is that he has no formal training in the administration of an educational system. He is not an educator or a scholar. But he does have over thirty years of experience in helping people become effective and productive citizens. And he recognizes the role that adults must play in teaching children self-discipline, both through the personal example that they set and by setting guidelines to which they hold the children, consistently and without fail.

"It's not my intention to turn our schools into boot camps," he says. "But that doesn't mean our students can't improve their mental attitude by learning to control their thoughts and behavior. The business of education is the same in or out of the army. It's about training the mind and the body. It's about succeeding through merit."

Stanford's plan has been to set the right example at the top, and through proper training, discipline, and fair play, pass the message on to the students. He started by asking fellow administrators to reallocate their work week so they spend one day per week working in the schools themselves. This could mean doing anything from tutoring students to helping clean and maintain the classrooms. He issued this directive because he wanted the central office staff to understand that the victory is in the classroom, to see the needs of the students firsthand, and to be reenergized by regular contact with their wonderful children.

Stanford expects his staff to answer telephone calls within the first three rings and to answer them politely. Punctuality has also been made the rule. Teachers are expected to be in their classrooms on time, and students must be seated and prepared to begin their lessons. A "snap to attention" is not necessary, but teachers and students are expected to be courteous and respectful with one another. Abusive language and behavior are not tolerated. Nor is an excuse tolerated for sloppy behavior inside or outside of the classroom.

In addition to setting higher personal and academic standards, Stanford has built a unique tracking system that requires teachers to file quarterly academic reports on every student in the system. Not only are the teachers held accountable but so are the parents of students, who Stanford believes should be graded on how well they encourage their children.

Students who excel are rewarded by being given privileges and honors. There are hopes that those students who want or need additional help will be invited to join academic "boot camps," which are still in the planning stages.

Stanford recognizes that his work with discipline-based education in the Seattle schools has just begun. "I don't have all the answers," he says. "No leader does. But I'm issuing a call to action."

The report card is still out on Stanford's approach to turning around the Seattle schools, but early indicators suggest his leadership is having an impact. He has also won the respect and loyalty of students, parents, school board members, business leaders, and administrators—no small accomplishment considering he has been on the job for such a short time.

As Colin Powell and Stanford clearly recognize, self-discipline is a key ingredient to a productive life. Without exercising self-discipline, we are unable to maintain our integrity—our ability to do what is right—and risk losing our personal freedom.

# PART II

# BECOMING FREE:
## Doing What We Want as Long as It Is the Right Thing to Do

Part of becoming free is becoming self-reliant. When we are self-reliant, or *not dependent* on others, we are not subject to their whims, opinions, decisions, actions, strengths, and weaknesses. From my point of view, the *only* dependence that can contribute to becoming free is dependence on and faith in God. When we submit to God we align ourselves with the Truth, and in doing so we are set free. Otherwise, dependence, whether it is on another person, an institution, or the state, is anathema to our own true freedom.

Also, when we are self-reliant, we do not impose a burden on others by depending upon them; thus we better uphold their freedom and rights. Therefore, although it is obvious that becoming free allows us to "do what we want," it is also one of the very best ways to "do what is right."

As previously noted, "doing what is right" requires abilities.

Many of the components of integrity presented in Part 1, including self-discipline, courage, humility, reasoning, and compassion, contribute to those abilities. But these same values also contribute to our ability "to do what we want." Indeed, as with "doing what is right," we must also have the *ability* "to do what we want." This leads us, perhaps, to a more complete definition of freedom: "having the ability to do what we want, the ability to do what is right, and doing both."

The values, or components, that I present in Part 2 contribute to becoming free—becoming self-reliant and doing what we want—by strengthening our abilities to do so. Optimism is the first and most obvious component of becoming free because so much else depends upon it.

## 9

# Optimism

Henry Ford, a great visionary, recognized the power of optimism when he said, "Whether you believe you will succeed or fail, you are right." He understood, perhaps better than most of us, how one's outlook on life has a lot to do with what one does with that life.

At Amway, we believe that optimism plays a very important role in the success of our business. It is our can-do attitude, the belief that we can overcome obstacles and reach our goals, that sets us apart as an organization. Our operative words are "Yes we can."

Many view optimism as a character trait that people are born with. I don't agree. I believe optimism is more of an attitude or a decision to view the world in a certain way. And the decision is ours. Changing the way we think definitely requires some self-awareness and self-discipline, but it is possible for everyone. And while optimism might be described as "seeing the world through rose-colored glasses," it is not to be confused with being blind to life's challenges. Optimism merely sees beyond the current challenge.

There is increasing scientific evidence to support the notion that our outlook plays a large role in how things go in our lives. Research among college students has shown that the level of optimism among freshmen at the beginning of their first semester at college is a more accurate predictor of their grades than their SAT scores or grade point average in high school. And optimistic salespeople sell more television sets and cars than their pessimistic counterparts.

If we are not optimistic about the outcome of what we do, we are far less likely to take initiative and get anything worthwhile done. We are more likely to act out of fear of losing what we have or fear of failure, subsequently wasting our talents, resources, and opportunities. We would never start a business if we thought we were going to end up broke. We probably wouldn't go to school if we thought we would have no opportunities to apply what we have learned. And it sure wouldn't make sense to get married if we honestly believed the marriage would end in divorce.

Optimists look past obstacles and view things as possible. They find a way to break through the barrier of naysayers and contrariness. If we see ourselves and the world around us in a positive light, we are much more likely to be ambitious. And if we feel hopeful in general, we are better able to deal with difficulties and setbacks.

Optimists are people who recognize that while they do not have control over every aspect of life, they do have control over themselves and how they react to life. They take

responsibility for themselves and therefore don't see themselves as victims. In short, optimists are more self-reliant.
They are also more likely to do what they truly want to do.

Let's take two tennis players as an example—one an optimist, the other a pessimist. The optimistic tennis player is just
as likely as any other to face a difficult opponent. Like a pessimist, an optimist can only play as well as his or her current
talent or skill level will allow. Yet the optimist, when losing a
game, leaves the court thinking of ways to improve the
chances of winning the next match. The pessimist is merely
disappointed by the loss. The optimist takes responsibility and
learns from the loss—an aid to future decisions that must be
made. The pessimist has nothing to learn because he or she
assumes the future is out of his or her hands. Looking at it
this way, pessimism is readily recognizable as self-indulgence.
Pessimists often see themselves as victims and are more likely
to feel sorry for themselves.

True-life examples of optimism at work are both plentiful
and memorable. At the Olympic Games in Seoul, South Korea,
the U.S. swimmer Matt Biondi was the odds-on favorite to win
seven gold medals, just as Mark Spitz had done sixteen years
earlier. But after Biondi turned in disappointing performances
in his first two races, most commentators thought he had lost
his edge. Psychologist Martin Seligman, author of a pioneering
study, *Learned Optimism*, did not agree. He had conducted
tests on Biondi, and the results had shown Seligman that
Biondi possessed an extraordinary positive and upbeat attitude. Rather than the losses lessening his chances, Seligman
predicted, Biondi would respond by performing even better.
And that is exactly what he did. He went on to win five gold
medals.

The story of Dave Johnson of the Baltimore Orioles is another inspiring example of optimism in action. Dave was unique in the world of pro baseball, having started out with the Orioles as a twenty-nine-year-old rookie pitcher, an oxymoron in baseball. Pitchers frequently arrive in their late teens or early twenties, red-hot and ready to take the sport by storm.

You might say Johnson was behind from the start. By his own estimation, he was not the most naturally gifted ballplayer to take the field. Never the fastest, the strongest, or the hardest thrower, he was always the last to be chosen for a school team. However, even as a boy, there lurked within him the stubborn belief that someday he would play for the Baltimore Orioles. It was this outlook, this optimistic hold on his ambitious dreams and goals, that made the difference.

The team Johnson played on in high school won the Baltimore County championship, and from then on Dave was never the same. He wanted to pitch college baseball at Essex Community College, but the competition from the up-and-coming high school pitchers was overwhelming. They were big guys who threw fast, and Johnson was just a five-ten, 135-pound right-hander. No chance.

Because he had to earn a living, he began driving an eighteen-wheel truck, but he still played ball in the county semipro league. When the big-league scouts came around, they always sang the same song about Dave: too small, too lightweight, not fast enough. "Get yourself a good ninety-mile-an-hour heater, kid, then come see us" was a familiar refrain.

Johnson couldn't help but be frustrated. He was striking guys out. He wasn't exactly sure how he struck them out, but an awful lot of them ended up walking back to the dugout when they were up against him. And that's what pitching ball was all about—getting guys out. He didn't understand why no one would give him a chance.

At age twenty, Johnson was offered a baseball scholarship to the Community College of Baltimore. He won eleven games, with no losses. The team ended up in the Junior College World Series, and the big-league scouts were there. Johnson thought this could be his big break.

Then he dropped the ball. Literally. At a crucial point in a crucial game, the umpire called a ball on him, and the winning run walked across home plate without so much as a bunt required. It seemed like a crushing bad break, but Johnson stayed positive. He wasn't about to throw in the towel.

Not long after that he was pitching for a sandlot team in Baltimore when he was approached by a baseball scout and invited out to dinner to discuss his future in professional baseball. The scout, Bob Dawson, though equally baffled at how Johnson got strikeouts, admitted that he saw something in Dave that he admired: determination. That meeting ended with Dave signing a contract with the Pittsburgh Pirates' minor-league team, the Salem Buccaneers. It seemed like a big break, but in reality it was just another small step on the long road back to Baltimore.

Along the way, Johnson married his childhood sweetheart, Tera, and started moving up through the minor leagues, from A ball to Double-A to Triple-A ball. He watched as other pitchers zipped past him on their way up, and equally fast, on their way down. Dave didn't let it shake him, though. Instead, he concentrated on being consistent, learning the finer points of his craft, and figuring out how to pitch the baseball into places over home plate where the batters either couldn't get at it in time or weren't sure where it was.

In one year Johnson won fifteen games for the Buffalo Bisons, a Triple-A team. But no one called him up to the majors. He signed with the Houston Astros organization, but was lost in a field of seven other dazzling pitchers. He never even got a start.

Then came the call he had been waiting years for! He'd been traded, and he was ordered to show up at the Baltimore Orioles' minor-league club in Rochester, New York.

Throughout the season, Johnson waited uneasily in the minors, watching as the Orioles moved up in the standings. Eventually it became clear that they would actually have a shot at the pennant.

Dave finally got the call from the Orioles. They wanted him to pitch the second game of a rain-threatened double-header in Boston. Dave knew that if the second game was rained out, he'd be sent back to Rochester and might never get a chance to pitch a single ball in the majors.

He watched and prayed. As the clouds parted and the umbrellas were put away, the legendary Frank Robinson, manager of the Orioles, walked up to Dave, handed him the ball, and said, "Go get 'em, kid."

Dave's first outing was a mixed one. One crucial play of the game came following a fastball Dave hung over the plate in front of notorious slugger Nick Esasky. Some of Dave's teammates claim that Esasky hit that ball so hard it hasn't landed yet. The mistake cost Baltimore four runs and, eventually, the game.

As they say, nobody is perfect. But a player in Dave's position, having just come up from the minors, couldn't afford a bad performance. The pressure was enormous. However, instead of folding under it, Dave showed the considerable skills he'd acquired over the years. He pitched quality ball for the next three innings, holding Boston hitless, before Robinson relieved him. Dave Johnson had survived his first big-league start.

In his next game for the Orioles, Dave not only lasted out the full nine innings, but led the team to a win before a home crowd in Baltimore's Memorial Stadium. He led his team to a win in his next game also. For that he was awarded the American League Player of the Week award.

That year, the Baltimore Orioles, the team Dave Johnson had wanted to play for his whole life, and of which he was now an important part, nearly won the pennant. And if they'd had a few more Dave Johnsons in their bullpen, they just might have.

It's apparent that Dave's optimism served not only himself but the team he played for. And his optimism may have helped more than his professional life; it may have helped him maintain his health also.

Hospital studies reveal that optimism plays a significant role in keeping us healthy. Optimistic patients, for example, require fewer antibiotics and are considerably less prone to heart attacks.

In contrast, tests also show that pessimists are more prone to depression and have more physical illnesses, from colds to cancer to heart disease. This could be because optimists are more likely to stick to health regimens and seek medical help when they are sick. But it also has a basis in the fact that the immune system is affected by stress. Whatever the reason, we know that optimistic heart patients recover faster after coronary bypass surgery, and that optimistic people generally heal faster.

Research also shows that an upbeat attitude isn't just something we are born with. It is a skill anyone can master. As Napoleon Hill, the late, great promoter of positive thinking points out, while our time and our labor may be subject to the demands of our family and employer, our mind is the one thing that cannot be controlled by anyone but ourselves. The thoughts that shape our attitudes toward our job, our abilities, our family, and our life in general are ours. We may choose to dwell on the reasons why a job can't be done, or we can look at all the ways we could do the job. That wonderful book *The Little Engine That Could,* which was read to me as a child and which I have read to my children, conveys this notion well.

While I accept that human nature is not perfect, I like to look beyond that. Rather than focus on other people's eccentricities, oddities, and quirks, it's important to focus on the good in them. My faith has everything to do with my optimism. For one thing, it is easier to take a positive view of life when we believe that the world was created and didn't just happen. If we believe that people were made special, with a purpose, and are not accidents of nature, and if we believe that there is a God watching over the world he made, then we can take comfort that ultimately things are going to turn out for the best, even though the results may not always occur when or how we want them to.

I believe that ultimately, good triumphs. God makes that possible. I am optimistic about the future because I believe He is in charge, eternal and there to help me when I am in need. And because Jesus sacrificed himself to gain our forgiveness, through faith and confession we *are* forgiven—mistakes are not held against us for eternity. We are not weighed down forever and can go forward with a clean slate—without our mistakes accumulating.

If instead I were a fatalist and thought there was no plan—if I believed that good probably won't triumph, or that there was no order to the world, no purpose to life, that my mistakes just accumulate against me, that there was no one there to help in times of need, and everything in the world was just a series of random events—I would have an overwhelming feeling of pessimism.

But because of my faith, I find myself an inherent and unabashed optimist—always tending to see the possibilities rather than the obstacles. Faith in the future not only creates optimism; it brings about hope. Hope can make life more livable and can even be necessary to our survival. An up-lifting story about the power of hope is told by Dr. Kenneth Swan, professor of surgery at the New Jersey Medical School.

Dr. Swan first met with Ken McGarity at the height of the Vietnam War when Dr. Swan was a young captain, four months out of surgical residency, stationed at the Seventy-first Evacuation Hospital outside Pleiku, in South Vietnam. He was eating dinner when an emergency call came in. An army helicopter had taken a direct hit from an enemy rocket. In the explosion, nineteen-year-old Ken McGarity had suffered severe injuries to his head, legs, and arms. As he lay on the stretcher, his blond hair caked with blood, the barely conscious patient kept reaching for the tangled mess of bone and tissue that had been his legs. "I think my legs are back on the chopper," he told Swan.

McGarity was wounded so severely, and his condition appeared so hopeless, that if the operating room had been filled with other wounded soldiers, Dr. Swan might have followed standard triage procedures and shunted him aside as the least likely to survive. The fact that McGarity was the only patient needing attention increased his chances for survival.

Dr. Swan's medical team worked on McGarity for seven hours. They managed to save his arms, but were forced to amputate both legs and one finger. An ophthalmologist removed his left eye and tried unsuccessfully to save his right eye. A neurosurgeon had to remove a large metal fragment from his brain, and many other wounds required treatment.

In a letter Dr. Swan wrote to his wife after the operation he confessed, "I couldn't believe he was alive and I didn't want him to be alive." But Dr. Swan did not doubt his responsibility to do what he could to save the man's life. The following day colleagues questioned his decision, pointing out that the patient's future looked dismal. Dr. Swan responded, "I was trained to take care of the sick and wounded. God will decide who lives or dies."

McGarity did survive and was sent to Japan to recover. Dr. Swan lost track of him after that. But when the chaplain's assistant at the Seventy-first Evacuation Hospital, with whom Dr. Swan played touch football, later reported that McGarity had been sent home, Dr. Swan was shocked by the realization that his patient had survived. The awful image of McGarity's life ahead raised serious doubts in Dr. Swan's mind as to whether he *had* done the right thing after all.

In fact, he was so tormented and traumatized by his grim vision of McGarity's future—maybe living out his life in a forsaken ward of a VA hospital somewhere, blind and perhaps drug-addicted—that Dr. Swan's mind blocked out all memory of him.

Then, nearly twenty-five years later, during an interview for an article on trauma care for the *American Medical News*, Peter MacPherson asked Dr. Swan to describe the worst injuries he had ever treated. It was only then that the memory of the horribly wounded soldier he had treated in Vietnam returned.

Subsequently, McGarity's story appeared in MacPherson's articles and readers responded by asking what had become of the soldier, speculating on whether Dr. Swan had done the right thing or not. It was at this point that Dr. Swan developed a great need to find the answer to those questions. His biggest problem was that he didn't remember McGarity's last name, only his first.

A search through the military records at the National Archives in Washington, D.C., proved fruitless. Then Mac-Pherson was shown a computer file from the Casualty Care Research Center's Wound Data and Munitions Effectiveness Team (WDMET), which, by sheer coincidence, had been conducting a study at the Seventy-first Evacuation Hospital at the time of the operation. Dr. Swan called the research center, and sure enough, they had the information he was looking for but were unwilling to release it. Two years went by before Dr. Swan was able to get that information.

He finally learned that his former patient was living in Columbus, Georgia, and decided to visit. When he found the address on a tree-lined street in a suburban neighborhood, McGarity's wife, Theresa, answered the door and welcomed him inside. She led him to the room where his former patient was waiting.

McGarity, now a stocky, balding man with a cheerful disposition and a heartwarming smile, wheeled over to Dr. Swan and shook his hand. In spite of his missing finger, McGarity's grip was strong.

"I'm pleased to meet you," McGarity said. "For the second time."

McGarity had come a long way since Vietnam. Among other skills, he had taught himself to play the piano, change diapers, fix flat tires, and even repair the roof on his house. He had returned to school, obtained his high school equivalency diploma, completed a year and a half of college, and was now raising two children while working at home part-time, helping to put his wife through school.

McGarity told the doctor that it had been hope that had pulled him through the hard times. After recuperating in Japan, he had woken up on his flight back to the United States and begun thinking of all the hopes and dreams he had—all the things he still wanted to do. More than anything else, he was thankful for the fact that he was still alive to do them.

McGarity first met his wife, Theresa, when he spoke to her over a citizens band radio. She wasn't put off by the fact that he was blind and disabled. Her maternal grandmother was blind, and she had a close school friend who had cerebral palsy and had been confined to a wheelchair throughout their childhood. The couple were married four months after they met in person at a picnic for CB enthusiasts.

"I always wanted to meet the man who saved Kenneth's

life," Theresa told Dr. Swan. "Thank you for these twenty wonderful years and for our two beautiful daughters."

Optimism and the hope that comes out of it can lead to a life worth living, even in the most difficult of circumstances. It was hope and optimism that made the difference between the helpless and dependent man Dr. Swan had envisioned and the fulfilled and self-reliant family man he actually met. I believe optimism gives us the outlook we need if we are to become truly free. For me that optimism is rooted in my faith, and the result is a positive attitude toward life.

## 10

# Commitment

Commitment is the second component of becoming free. Becoming free does not mean that we only have the ability to make choices. We must also commit ourselves to making the correct choices and to doing what is right. If we do not want to spend our lives like a boat adrift, then we must pledge to keep our word and do what we say we are going to do. Like setting goals, for instance. Setting goals is a very important step for each of us to take, but what's the use unless you're committed to their fulfillment? When we set goals, we are taking the first step toward doing what we want and becoming self-reliant. Doing what is right is making the commitment to achieving our goals.

Goals can be different for each person. One person may pursue her love of teaching and do what she is called to, becoming self-reliant in the process. In contrast, another may take on teaching because she simply needs a job, not because she is committed to that profession.

The goals for each of us can be as unique as we are. The biblical teaching is that each of us has some work to do in God's service. That work is as varied as the unique gifts that God has given each of us. I believe that our chief task in life is to fulfill that purpose. Some people discover their purpose in childhood, and others spend their lives searching for it. If we don't know how we should spend our time, it is helpful to look at the talents and abilities that seem to come easily to us. We must also look into our hearts to discover our calling, whether it is to care for children, to teach, to heal, create, organize, or coordinate, to solve problems, or to lead. If we look back over our life experiences, we can determine when we have been the most fulfilled. Or we can consult with family members and friends, who may also have insights into our gifts. We must also have goals and a personal vision to strive toward their fulfillment.

While goals we set play a crucial part in becoming free, there is much more to it than that. We must commit ourselves to achieving those goals if we are to do what is right. As an adult, a spouse, or a parent, having our own home to live in, food on the table, and a happy family life are laudable goals. Whether we strive to be community leaders, active citizens, responsible co-workers, or diligent students—all are worthy goals that will help us in becoming free, but only if we are committed to seeing them through.

Often we find that upon reaching our individual goals we rise to a new plateau and our vision to see even greater opportunity expands. This enables us to reach for higher goals. For example, we might have the goal of owning a home. Once we achieve that goal we may want to set new goals, such as renovating or redecorating our home, or even relocating to a new home. These are commendable goals, but not practical unless we make the personal commitment to achieve them.

Commitment means making a pledge or promise to pour one's energies and resources into succeeding at one's goal and keeping one's word. A family friend has described commitment as reaching out to our future and establishing an oasis of certainty. He also describes it as a form of love—a deliberate bonding of oneself to another. For me, my first commitment is to God, followed by my commitment to my wife Betsy and our children.

Unfortunately, today, the word "commitment" is often used to suggest an obligation that we have entered into unwittingly, in essence suggesting we have fallen asleep at the wheel.

As an example, people sometimes marry without consciously committing themselves to their spouse or to the responsibility of a family. In many cases, the prospective partners haven't even stopped to think about their personal commitments, let alone their common commitments.

Fulfilling our commitments requires integrity. It requires being honest with ourselves and others, and being reliable, thoughtful, and fair. We must also depend on self-discipline and courage if we are going to make and fulfill commitments that lead us to greater freedom.

If we are to become free, we ourselves must set goals and commit ourselves to achieving them in all areas of life—as a spouse, sibling, child or parent, as a church member, citizen, or neighbor, or as a fellow student or worker.

The truth is, the nature of our commitment and the degree to which we are committed to reaching our goals can be evidenced only through our actions.

Actions do speak louder than words. For example, a man may say he is committed to his wife and family, but if he is working eighty hours a week and spending the rest of his time on the golf course, his real commitment is actually quite clear.

Fulfilling our commitments is of great importance. While committing to doing what we want may be one priority, *doing* what is right is not only more important, but necessary to fulfilling God's plan for our lives.

The story of Bill Havens, from McLean, Virginia, illustrates how commitments may conflict. An amateur athlete and a devoted husband, Bill was faced with the difficulty of choosing between being with his wife for the birth of their first child or fulfilling his life's dream by competing in the Olympics.

Bill's story took place many years ago, when the Olympic Games were held in Paris and canoe racing was featured for the first time. Bill had begun canoe racing years earlier and had been committed to training for this one opportunity. But as the time drew near, his wife was due to deliver their first child. Despite her encouragement to go and fulfill his dreams, Bill remained behind to keep his commitment to her and their young family.

As it turned out, the baby arrived late and Bill, who could have gone after all and still been there for the birth, missed the opportunity of a lifetime. His team won the gold medal without him.

However, Bill did not become bitter about this, nor did he

take out his disappointment on his wife and child. Instead, he passed on his love of canoe racing to his son, Frank. And he could not have been more pleased when, twenty-eight years later, he received a telegram from Helsinki, announcing that Frank was bringing home the gold medal for canoe racing!

Bill's commitment to his sport was never in question. The Olympic goal was important to him. But his commitment to his marriage and his family was clearly more important. For Bill, fulfilling the greater commitment was the right thing to do.

Commitment means more than just setting a goal or making a promise. It means throwing ourselves into keeping that commitment with passion, energy, and total commitment.

Americans are known for their inventiveness. However, what has made America great is not just having good ideas, but the commitment to making those ideas reality. In my hometown of Grand Rapids, Michigan, the idea of building a large community arena had been discussed for ten or fifteen years. But it wasn't until a few community members, myself included, got together and firmly decided we were going to find a way to make it happen, that it had any hope of becoming a reality. We didn't know where the money was going to come from, and we were up against naysayers who claimed it couldn't work. But we felt it was the right thing to do, so we set the goal and worked toward it. One way or another we were going to make it happen. We were committed enough to openly support the building of the arena and risk public criticism. We did succeed in getting people together. As a result, our community now enjoys world-class sports and entertainment in a beautiful new arena.

There is no doubt that goal setting and a high level of commitment, combined with integrity, can accomplish almost anything. Just ask Eula Hall, who operates a free medical clinic in an area in Kentucky called Mud Creek.

Born and raised in rural eastern Kentucky, with only five years of schooling, Eula began her work among the poorest of the Appalachian poor after having raised five children of her own. As the newly elected head of the health committee in a local welfare-rights organization, Eula decided to take as her first challenge cleaning up the drinking water in the Mud Creek Water District. Over the years, hepatitis, typhus, and dysentery had become the norm. But accepting the worst of life was not in Eula's character. And she knew where the problem was—in the wells. But she had to prove it before she could get it fixed.

Eula recruited volunteers from the University of Kentucky Medical School, local high schools, and hospital personnel to collect samples for analysis. Her suspicions were validated— the water from ninety percent of the district's wells was not fit to drink. Armed with this evidence, she talked the local government into drilling deeper wells, and got over sixty miles of new water supply pipes installed. Now, nearly a thousand families in Mud Creek are supplied with safe drinking water.

Having tackled that problem so successfully, Eula turned her attention to the issue of medical care. This had long been a problem in Mud Creek, and she had seen too many of her friends and relatives go to the graveyard young. It was easy to see why: the nearest clinic was over twenty miles away, and it was difficult for most people to get there.

Eula opened her first clinic in nearby Tinker Fork. It was actually nothing more than a trailer operated by volunteers and supplied by money donated by the United Mine Workers. The vast majority of patients were coal miners in the throes of black lung disease, acquired from years of breathing the coal-dust-laden air of the mines. The clinic was well under way and meeting an important need when it caught fire and burned. Deeply saddened, but undeterred, Eula set up shop on a picnic table under a willow tree. The first day after the fire, Eula had a doctor, a list of patients, a small pharmacy, and a working telephone.

The media were quick to spread the word about the unusual Mud Creek Clinic, named after the nearby stream, and the amazing commitment of a woman named Eula Hall. Within a few months, with donations from both public and private sources, she was able to acquire a building for the clinic, which was operated by a full complement of professionals: two doctors, two pharmacists, four nurses, a lab technician, a physician's assistant, an X-ray technician, a social director, and clerical staff to administer the records and admissions procedures. And, as always, the volunteers.

Today, inspired by Eula's commitment, doctors come from all over, sometimes for a month at a time, to donate their services. No one who seeks help has ever been turned away, and not long ago, the clinic handled over four thousand patients in one year.

The power of commitment, as Eula Hall is quick to acknowledge, "is potent medicine." As any committed person knows, the mere courageous act of stepping across the line, of boldly standing up to be counted, or giving oneself to a worthy cause positively impacts and sets an example for others.

People who make and keep commitments take control of

their lives. They make promises and then they keep them. They set goals and they commit to achieving them. In doing so, they become more self-reliant; and thus they become more free, serving as a constant encouragement and example for others.

## 11

# Initiative

When we fulfill our commitments, we determine our destination. As noted in the previous chapter, getting where we want to go does not just mean making commitments; we must also keep them. Initiative, the third component of becoming free, is necessary to start us moving toward fulfilling the commitments we make.

Taking initiative means overcoming our resistance to change, getting rid of excuses, and overcoming procrastination. Like everything else we have discussed, taking initiative requires a good measure of self-discipline. And because beginnings are really the hardest, courage is also important. When we take our first steps the results are never certain, so we must be willing to take risks and can't be afraid to look foolish.

The Amway Corporation was built on the idea that people

can have and are willing to take initiative. No one could question the initiative that Dad and Jay took, despite being told on many occasions how foolish their idea was. Nor can anyone question the initiative now shown by so many in our organization, especially Amway distributors.

It also took initiative for me to leave the comfort zone of our established and thriving family business when Betsy and I started up our own company. But it was important to do this in order to gain the greater experience and the broader perspective that comes from working in a small company, where I didn't have the security of being in an established family business.

Often I hear people say that there is no point in taking initiative because all the good opportunities have already been taken. Sentiments like this have been voiced since long before the advent of the industrial revolution, mass transportation, mass media, and the information superhighway.

Taking initiative often involves being creative. That's the nature of entrepreneurial insight. It is not just doing what others are unable or unwilling to do. This kind of initiative calls for vision, the ability to see what others are unable to see. Wayne Gretzky demonstrates this when he skates to where the puck is going to be rather than where it is.

Or you may have heard the story of the boy who sat for days watching in awe as a sculptor carved a beautiful figure out of marble. When the sculptor was finally finished and the boy realized what it was, he gasped and said, "How did you know it was in there?"

My father showed this kind of vision when he stood in front of the old building that eventually became the elegant and flourishing Grand Plaza Hotel in Grand Rapids.

If Henry Ford, the Wright brothers, or Thomas Edison had not had this kind of vision and initiative, our world would be very different today. And it would be very different today if our founding fathers had not had the vision of a nation built on the notion of liberty.

Usually we recognize initiative when someone has gone up against considerable odds to accomplish his or her goals. But that isn't what most of us need to do on an everyday basis. Some of us just need to get out of a rut. It may be one that we created ourselves, one we were born into, or one that we fell (or maybe feel we were pushed) into. Regardless of how we got there, getting out requires taking a first step. That first step doesn't have to be significant; it just needs to be a step that takes us in the right direction. And once we take it, the second is a little easier, and the third is easier still.

A woman who took the initiative to take the first step is Bessie Pender, from Norfolk, Virginia, a fifth-grade teacher at the Coleman Place Elementary School. What makes her story so interesting is that she got her start in the Norfolk public schools not as a teacher but as a janitorial assistant, a position she held for seventeen years.

Pender remembers the moment she made the decision to fulfill her lifetime dream of becoming a teacher. She had just begun her cleaning rounds at the Larrymore Elementary School when she walked into the fifth-grade classroom. The room was a disaster. Papers were scattered all over the room. The school desks were shoved out of their rows. Fingerprints covered the windows, and the blackboard was a mess.

"I wasn't ashamed of my work," Pender says. "Cleaning is a good, honest living, and doing it for schools is a way to contribute to the betterment of children. But I knew as I looked across that classroom that I could make a bigger contribution. I knew I could be a teacher. Perhaps not the best. But I knew I had it in me."

That day, Pender put down her mop and called a telephone number she had seen in the teachers' lounge. It was the number for a teachers' college, which responded by mailing Pender an application. She filled it out, sent it in, and within two weeks found herself enrolled in the program that eventually led to her teaching degree. But getting there wasn't easy. Pender, who was older than most of her instructors, had to work full-time and take care of her teenage daughter, on top of her schooling. It took her seven years to get her degree.

"But I did it," Pender says. "And you can do it too," she tells her students.

As Pender's story illustrates, the initiative to take that first step is generated from within. We can all have goals as did Bessie, but it's not until we take the first step that we have any hope of reaching that goal—even if it takes us seven years to do it.

Initiative is a quality that human resource managers prize. It differentiates the people who come to work to watch things happen from those who come to work to make things happen.

Initiative is something that's impossible to fake. We either have it or we don't, although that doesn't mean it can't be developed. Being highly creative helps, but it's not the only factor. We can have an abundance of ideas, but the level of initiative determines what we do with those ideas or how real those ideas become.

Initiative is an important aspect of being a Christian, as we must sometimes take the initiative not in response to an inner desire but in response to a "call" or a commandment. We have received the gift of life and are called to make something of that life. And as James teaches us in the New Testament, "faith without works is dead." The biblical parable of the talents describes this well. Three servants were each given some talents (money) by their master to invest on his behalf. One did nothing but bury his. The other two took initiative and actively went out and invested their talents. In doing so, they were able to add to them. When the master returned, the first servant was able to give back only what he had been given, while the other two returned double what they had received. The master, pleased with the faithfulness of these two with "just a few things," subsequently made them ruler over many. But he took away the talent from the servant who had only buried his, and gave it to one of the others. As this parable illustrates, it is only through our actions and the initiative we take that we can demonstrate our faith.

There is no "one size fits all" formula to exhibiting initiative. Our goals and motivations are different and may very well change over the years. A young father might show initiative by taking time away from his career to spend a few more hours each week with his family. A fifty-year-old mother might demonstrate initiative by going back to work or school after her children have left the nest.

Taking initiative requires us to convert passive feelings into active ones. Optimism and commitment are necessary, as is overcoming the fear of failure. All too often we let our desire for perfection or our fear of failure stand in the way of moving ahead with a new initiative. I recall that my father was always fond of saying, "If at first you don't succeed, try, try again."

Another type of initiative is seeing or recognizing a need before others do, and acting upon it. This could be something as simple as picking up a piece of paper on the office floor that others have just walked over, or something as important as discovering more efficient ways to feed a growing population. Without this kind of initiative there would be very little progress. We would likely be living in primitive conditions yet today without many of the comforts or conveniences modern life affords us.

It is this type of initiative that scientist John Jeavons has taken. Ever since his graduation from Yale, through his early career at the Agency for International Development, and then at Stanford University, Jeavons has been taking the steps to find out exactly how much (or more precisely, how little) space on this planet it takes to provide food, shelter, and necessary income for one human being. And equally important, he has studied how the negative environmental impact of providing for one person's needs can be minimized or even transformed into something positive. Today's ever-increasing global population, limited arable land, crop failures, and the attendant famines add a tangible urgency to Jeavons's lifetime quest for down-to-earth answers for our future.

Early on in his career, Jeavons concluded that inefficient land use and depleted resources were hallmarks of our times. In his search for solutions to this problem, a respectful look back to ancient traditional farming methods provided a good starting point for Jeavons. Past civilizations are rich depositories of information, and he borrowed liberally from them, forming the foundation of an effective and environmentally sound miniaturization of agriculture that has come to be known as "biointensive minifarming." Developed in the

United States, this is a concept that is now being taught around the world. Jeavons is currently doing this work with Ecology Action in Willits, California.

The method espoused by Jeavons utilizes much smaller tracts of arable land than those used by modern agriculture, yet boasts harvests that eclipse those commonly achieved today. Increases of two to six times the yield are reported, and his methods actually enrich the soil rather than deplete it, make far better use of available water supplies, and have a fraction of the usual pest and disease problems.

The balance Jeavons seeks to strike is between productive use of the land on the one hand, and its conservation for future use on the other. "It's possible to take care of all the needs of the people," Jeavons contends, "while still leaving five-ninths of the earth's land surface in the wild. This is crucial for the maintenance of plant and animal genetic diversity."

Jeavons has gotten impressive results in his research, providing answers to many of his original questions, most notably how much land is required for one person to live. The good news is that in a six-month growing season, a mere four hundred square feet can provide a family of four with all the vegetables and fruits they'll need for one year. In addition, one person should be able to grow *all* of his or her own food on as little as four thousand square feet. This is one-tenth of the forty-two thousand square feet of land now farmed for food on their behalf.

During his twenty-five years of research, Jeavons and his organization have published over thirty books, pamphlets, booklets, and manuals on the subject. His texts, curricula, training sessions, and lectures around the world provide him with opportunities to address the needs of the world's population and spread the word of the means at our disposal to meet them.

For years, Jeavons conducted his inquiry on his own initiative, in a field that didn't, until recently, take his ideas all that seriously. He investigated theories, studied history, questioned commercial farmers, and processed endless statistics. He took this initiative without any promise of professional recognition or financial remuneration. But when he looked up from his desk, so to speak, he found himself to be the recognized expert in his field.

"It was a case of 'Tag! You're it!' " an amused Jeavons recounts. "But over the years, I've become convinced that it's absolutely necessary for each and every one of us to do whatever we can. So, in a greater sense," Jeavons adds soberly, "it's 'tag,' we're all 'it.' "

As Jeavons has so aptly suggested, it is up to all of us to take initiative in our lives—whether it is to set about achieving our goal of making a difference in the lives of a group of fifth graders, as in the case of Bessie Pender, or to set about changing the course of history, as Jeavons may well do. Taking initiative gets us one step closer to becoming free.

## 12

# Work

As old-fashioned as it may sound, work is a necessary part of keeping our commitments, and it is essential to becoming free. After reading the stories about Bessie Pender and John Jeavons, no one could doubt that they had to work to accomplish their goals.

The term "work" doesn't just mean holding a job. It refers to activities that produce something, improve something, or better people's lives. Work includes the daily effort of raising children or cleaning a floor as well as designing a new marketing strategy, making tiles for the space shuttle, or leading an army into battle. Each activity is a form of work and should be meaningful and rewarding.

The writer Studs Terkel defined work in this way: "Work is about daily meaning as well as daily bread . . . for recognition as well as cash . . . for astonishment rather than torpor . . . for a sort of life rather than a Monday through Friday sort of dying." I believe that work is good only if it leads the worker to freedom, reward, recognition, and hope. In other words, work must be satisfying psychologically and spiritually as well as financially.

The idea that work in and of itself can be meaningful and rewarding is sometimes lost on people. And given the fact that more of our time is spent at our jobs or traveling to and from our jobs than in any other activity, it is unfortunate when the jobs don't provide joy or fulfillment.

It may seem silly to take time to define "work," because it's a word each of us frequently uses. This, however, is all the more reason to do so, because we often use it without really comprehending its true meaning. Perhaps if we were to better understand the dynamics of work, we would better understand and appreciate its value.

Work involves energy. The word "energy" comes from the Latin *energon*, which is composed of *en*, which means "at," and *ergon*, which means "work." In the field of physics, work is described simply as the "transfer of energy from one system to another."

If we were to think of work as a transfer of energy, and apply this concept to our everyday lives, then much of what we do would be categorized as work. If you studied physics, you might remember that energy cannot be created or destroyed, it can only be transferred or transformed. Even when we are simply breathing, sleeping, or moving, we use energy. In order to keep breathing and moving we must replace the energy we use with the food we eat. In order to provide the body with food, we must either sow, nurture, and harvest the food, or earn the money to buy it. Those activities obviously expend more energy, which then must be replaced. Thus, it becomes clear that our "daily work" is but one link in a cycle of energy transfer.

One may wonder if life is worthwhile if we just eat to live, live to work, and work to eat. It all sounds very uninspiring. Our pets may be content to lead their lives this way, but it is not, for the most part, something that most human beings would find particularly exciting.

All work can and should be meaningful. Some people speak of important jobs and menial jobs, but the success of any organization or effort depends on the contributions made by different individuals fulfilling different responsibilities. Work that is fulfilling for one person may not be fulfilling for another. The attitude we bring to work plays an important role in our enjoyment of and our ability to fulfill the task. If, when short-order cooks are preparing hamburgers, they can remember that what they are doing is feeding families; if while emptying bedpans, hospital orderlies recognize that they are playing a role in healing people; and if autoworkers are aware that they are not just working on an assembly line but offering safety and mobility to fellow citizens, then their work takes on greater meaning.

If our attitude toward our work is right and we still don't derive satisfaction from it, it may be that what we are doing does not line up with our God-given talents. I believe that we are called by God to utilize the skills He gave us to perform certain kinds of work. When we perform our work with integrity, it becomes a form of ministry. My faith teaches me that all work should be done for the glory of God. Therefore, all work is significant regardless of its financial reward.

A man who understands the transformational power of

work is Willie Gary, an inspirational public speaker, devoted husband, and gifted trial attorney. The framed diplomas on the walls of his office in Stuart, Florida, are a testament to his work as a scholar and jurist. A look at his hands, however, reveals his humble origins. He has known hard physical work, and plenty of it. He is a man, one might say, who realized early on that his best friends were his own hands.

The son of migrant farmworkers, Gary grew up with ten brothers and sisters in the back of a stake truck. There were peaches to harvest in Georgia, apples to pick in North Carolina, and beans to pick in Florida. All there was to life, it seemed, was hard work.

Like other children of migrants, Gary attended school in the mornings and worked with his parents in the afternoons. "There was no such thing as day care," he says, "only field care. That's the older children watching the younger children so they stay out of the way of the adults."

Rather than resent the hours he spent in the steaming hot fields, Gary was grateful for the opportunity to help out, because his contribution directly translated into tangible rewards at the dinner table. "You quickly learned the value of a day's labor, of helping yourself and making your own way."

From his many aunts and uncles, who routinely joined his family for Sunday services, which were delivered from a pulpit made of stacked packing crates under a shade tree at the edge of a farmer's field, he was also taught to play by the rules, to treat people the way he expected to be treated, and to help his fellow man.

Gary's father, more than anyone else, taught him about working hard. "My dad didn't know what giving up was all about," Gary remembers. "No matter what it was, tilling the soil, picking fruit, or selling melons from the back of a truck, he did it better and longer than anyone else. He grew the best crops, picked the most fruit, got the best prices. . . . It was all right to make mistakes, but you had to get back up and keep trying. The true champions always got back up off the mat."

By the time Gary reached his sixteenth birthday his father had saved enough money to buy a small bean farm outside of Indianhead, Florida. Gary still helped some on the farm, but now he was enrolled in high school and was expected to work hard in the classroom and on the football field. By sheer hard work he did well in both, but neither his grades nor his athletic ability was enough to get him a scholarship to college.

Every school Gary applied to turned him down for a scholarship. After he repeatedly asked his teachers for help, his football coach managed to arrange for an interview at Shaw College in Raleigh, North Carolina.

When Gary stepped off a Greyhound bus in Raleigh, with a suitcase tied closed with a rope, all his family's hopes and dreams were riding with him. No other African-American man from Indianhead, Florida, had ever attended college.

Gary's hopes were soon dashed when he discovered that the football coach he had been sent to see didn't seem to know why he had come, and wasn't interested in the details.

"I'm really sorry," the coach said. "I don't have an opening."

Gary had no money to get home, or even to make a telephone call. Unsure of where to go, he visited the dorm where the football players lived, hoping they might sneak him some food from the cafeteria. He spent the night on a sofa in the lounge.

Gary didn't feel right about living off handouts in the school dorm, so the next morning he decided he was going to work for his keep, even if he didn't get paid. He followed the football players into the locker room. After they had suited up and left for the field, he straightened up their clothes, put the supplies away, and washed the floors. Later, when the players returned from the game, showered, and left, he cleaned up again.

The assistant coach told the coach what was happening, and the coach called Gary into his office.

"I've heard you're doing a good job in the locker room," the coach said. "Here's a meal ticket. It's the least I can do."

The next day Gary helped the trainer carry equipment onto the field. Again, the coach took him aside. He asked where Gary was sleeping. Gary lied and said that he had a place to stay.

"No you don't," the coach corrected him. "I'll get you a bed in one of the dorms until the end of the week. Then you'll have to go home."

Gary thought he had reached the end of the line when football practice was over on Friday afternoon. He had no job prospects, and although he had filled out an application to the college, he hadn't been able to pay the fee to submit it. When the assistant coach told him that the head coach wanted to see him, Gary expected to be told that he had to give up his meal ticket and vacate the dorm room. But the coach surprised him.

"I'm glad you didn't go home," the coach said. "A linebacker has been hurt during practice. You can have his spot if you want it."

The uniform they gave Gary was too big for him, but he quickly grew into it. And his hard work paid off, on the field and in the classroom. Not only was Gary the first African-American student in his hometown to get a degree, he was the first black student from his hometown to even go to college.

With help from college faculty members, Gary applied and was accepted to law school at North Carolina Central University. Again, he poured every ounce of his energy into working hard. And three years later, Gary, now married to his childhood sweetheart, became the first black lawyer to practice in Stuart, Florida.

Soon, however, Gary began to wonder if all his hard work was for nothing. No matter how much he advertised, or what credentials he had to offer, he couldn't get a paying client. But he decided he wouldn't let that stop him. He would provide his services free of charge to anyone who needed his help.

Eventually, Gary's clients started paying him, and his practice got so busy that he had to take on partners. Today, Gary's firm is one of the most successful legal practices in the state of Florida. In fact, his practice is so prosperous, and Gary is so grateful for the help he received from Shaw College, that recently he donated $10 million to endow scholarships, hire faculty, and support a building fund for that school.

By utilizing his God-given talents, having the courage to press on, and remaining committed to his goals, Gary was fulfilling his life's purpose.

My parents gave me a firm foundation when they taught me the joy of utilizing my God-given talents and working to the best of my ability. And no matter how menial the task seemed, it was significant, whether I was weeding the flower beds or scrubbing the bathroom floor. Now having been blessed with success, I must work even harder to achieve new goals. In fact, like many today, I find that I have the tendency to go over the edge with work. However, I have learned it is important to keep our work in balance with the rest of our life and to be careful that we don't define ourselves only by the work we do.

I strongly believe the significance of what we do is not limited to the hours we spend at "work." Our commitment in every area of endeavor brings a unique meaning and completeness to our lives. This was certainly true for ecologist John Beal.

When Beal decided to clean up Seattle's Hamm Creek, most people who knew him would have agreed that he was not the kind of person anyone would put in charge of a fifty-five-square-mile watershed. He was a high school dropout, a former rodeo cowboy, a Vietnam veteran with post-traumatic stress disorder, and an armchair environmentalist. He hadn't held a steady job in more than a decade. And two heart attacks, a motorcycle accident resulting in a head injury and epilepsy, and the diagnosis of post-traumatic stress disorder, all within a period of one year, had convinced doctors that he had only a few months to live.

Beal didn't let this stop him. He knew no one would trust him with the restoration of Hamm Creek, so he took the job on himself, asking nothing more for his efforts than the pleasure of leaving this tributary of the Duwamish River a little better off than when he found it.

"I guess I had come to the point in my life when I looked back and saw that I hadn't contributed much to this world. You might say, I had left the world a lot worse off than the way

I found it. The only reason I chose Hamm Creek was because it was so close to my house and in such bad shape."

At the time, almost everyone had written Hamm Creek off as nothing more than a drainage ditch carrying factory runoff and residential waste into the befouled Duwamish River. So neighbors stood on the banks and gawked as Beal began his work. First he dragged a discarded refrigerator out of the muck. Next came tires, old television sets, scrap metal, paint cans, car parts, and an assortment of other waste. In less than a year he had dragged over one ton of trash out of the creek. City authorities carted away the first load as Beal tackled another section of the creek.

Beal had expected to be dead of a heart attack before he could finish cleaning the trash out of the creek, but the heart attack didn't come, so he decided to beautify the creek by planting grass and small trees and shrubs along its edges. Once his beautification plan was under way, he put some crayfish in the water. They died almost instantly.

"I suppose that's when I had to get serious about what I was doing. Before that, all the changes were cosmetic. Now I had to deal with the fact that the stream water itself was poisonous. I didn't think I was going to be able to reverse something that was fifty years in the making, but I decided at least to give it a try."

He first had to deal with all the oil and petroleum products that were polluting the creek. The plants and ground cover he had installed along the banks did some good, but not nearly enough. Amateur investigating revealed that a company was paying a contractor to dump its petroleum by-products directly into the river on a regular basis. Beal confronted the truck driver, who said, in effect, "I need the money." The manager who hired the contractor echoed similar sentiments. "My company won't be competitive if I pay to have the waste recycled."

Beal knew that calling the authorities wasn't going to solve the problem. Besides, neighbors would lose their jobs if he caused the company to be shut down. So Beal decided to find an economic solution that was right for the business as well as for the creek. The solution came in the form of a recycling co-op in which business operators pooled their petroleum by-products to be resold later. The idea caught on in a major way.

"As soon as the business owners saw they could save money and save Hamm Creek, there was no longer an issue. They all fell in line."

Later, these same companies became Beal's supporters as he tackled the problem of pollutants draining into the creek from city streets and parking lots. He certainly couldn't take the cars off the street, so he devised a unique filtration system that collected runoff oil in synthetic "booms" that floated on the creek's surface. The only problem was what to do with the oil once it had collected in the boom. Again, Beal used his initiative. He discovered the solution growing right on the banks of the creek: buttercups.

Beal had noticed that while other plants couldn't survive the toxic environment on the banks of the Hamm, these delicate and colorful yellow flowers flourished. "They literally drink up the oil," Beal reported. "I had only to plant them on the booms."

Again, Beal tried to put crayfish in the Hamm. And again they died, but this time it took ten days. "There was still something wrong," Beal said. "And I thought I knew what it was."

Beal took a soil sample from the streambed to the University of Seattle for analysis. Just as he had suspected, the soil itself was contaminated with high levels of heavy metal that had accumulated since the turn of the century. Beal experimented with shoveling sections of the creek bottom into drums, but the cost of disposing of it became prohibitive. He solved his problem, instead, by sinking low-level electromagnets into the streambed. The magnets collected the heavy metals, which he then turned over to a cement company. They, in turn, poured the contaminants into concrete.

"I was astonished at how quickly we got the stream cleaned up. At first, no one I told would believe it because they didn't think it was possible to reverse so many years of neglect. The evidence, of course, was the stream itself."

First the water bugs and crayfish returned. Then a pair of red-tailed hawks, hand-raised and introduced by Beal, set up a home on the creek's banks. Beal also introduced foxes, moles and voles, and many species of ants. The real thrill, however, came when coho salmon, planted in the creek, returned to spawn. The entire venture has been so successful that hundreds of schoolchildren and environmental groups have embraced Beal's efforts. The technology and methods he brought to Hamm Creek are now being used on five other streams, two lakes, and the entire Duwamish River. Environmental groups have taken the same technology to Russia and India.

Seventeen years after Beal began his cleanup, the mud from Hamm Creek is so pure that it is being used at some exclusive health clubs and resorts. "Promoters are calling this the healing waters of Hamm Creek," Beal says.

They may be right. His initiative and hard work have

restored the land and given him a new lease on life. What a tremendous example of remaining committed to a goal and persevering to get the job done.

Unfortunately, many children today have not learned the value of work. A few generations ago, children worked alongside their parents; the participation of a child was expected. When a child is not taught the value of helping attain family goals, the actual process of work is divorced from its end result. For instance, work becomes an abstract notion when a child believes that money comes from a cash machine at the bank. This was certainly not the case when children apprenticed under their parents. Many of today's children don't experience completion of a job, or feel the surge of pride that comes with it. Oftentimes the experiences they have with work are the assorted tasks or chores that parents assign them, and the only motivation they have is fear of being punished or being called lazy if they don't comply. The idea that work can be passionate, spontaneous, and fun is often missing from the equation.

If we are going to help our children to become self-reliant and fulfill their life's purpose, we are going to have to teach them the joy and dignity of work.

No matter what it is that we do, whether on the job, in our marriage, at school, in our place of worship, or in our community, we must be advancing God's work. The Hebrews called this *shalom*. In the Bible, *shalom* is described as universal flourishing, wholeness, and delight, or simply peace. It's the way things ought to be. Everything that we do could and should contribute in some way to this goal. It is the biggest "work" project in the universe, and we are called to preserve and accomplish the task.

# 13

# Perseverance

No matter what goals we set, what commitments we make, how much initiative we show, or how hard we work, if we don't persevere in striving toward our goals, we will never reach them. Accomplishing our goals is essential to securing individual freedom, and that's why perseverance is an important component of becoming free.

There is truth in the saying "You never win if you don't play," or more strongly stated, "Winners never quit and quitters never win." In a survey conducted by the *Los Angeles Times*, researchers interviewing 120 of the top performers in business, sports, politics, entertainment, and academia found that talent was only a small part of what had enabled them to reach the top in their fields. In fact, the parents of top performers revealed that their children had far exceeded expectations. Mothers often remarked that a sibling initially had shown more talent than the child who eventually reached the pinnacle in his or her profession. The single thing the top performers had in common was how persistently they worked to reach the top.

The life story of the late Orville Redenbacher is a classic example of perseverance. All of us have heard his name. He's America's popcorn king. Few people, however, know the struggle he had selling his first jar of popcorn.

Redenbacher was the first to admit how close he came to being a complete failure in the popcorn business. By the age of sixty-three he had spent a decade and many thousands of dollars crisscrossing the country, pursuing what nearly everyone thought to be a foolish dream: selling hybrid speciality popcorn at nearly two and a half times the regular price. Buyers at supermarkets all had the same reaction: No one would be willing to pay more than the going rate. Yet Redenbacher persisted.

"It may sound corny," he was fond of saying, "but anything worth having is worth striving for with all your might. Be persistent. That's all there is to it. There are no magic formulas."

Redenbacher's idea for selling speciality popping corn had been formulated over a long period of time. As a child of a farmer in Brazil, Indiana, he enjoyed the warm, homey aroma of the popcorn his father would make nightly in a long-handled wire popper over a potbellied stone. It was his favorite snack. To earn spending money, twelve-year-old Redenbacher would hike fifteen miles to the city of Terre Haute twice a week to sell fruit, vegetables, eggs, and dressed chickens from their farm. But of all the produce he sold door to door, popping corn interested him the most. In fact, he raised it himself as a 4-H project on an acre of his father's land. Each year he tried to improve on a formula that had remained virtually the same since the Iroquois Indians had introduced popping corn to colonialists 250 years earlier.

Redenbacher received an appointment to West Point, but he attended Purdue University instead, so he could major in agronomy. Upon graduation, he became the Virgo County agricultural agent in Terre Haute, where he had the novel idea of broadcasting his agricultural reports directly from corn-fields. Next he became manager of the twelve-thousand-acre Princeton Farms, where he began breeding hybrid popcorn seed using liquid nitrogen.

Later, Redenbacher teamed up with fellow Purdue gradu-ate Charlie Bowman, and they bought Chester, Incorporated, a diversified agricultural company in Valparaiso, Indiana. While Bowman concentrated on developing grain storage and irriga-tion systems. Redenbacher continued experimenting with vari-ous hybrid popping corns and fertilizers. Eventually, with the help of breeding expert Carl Hartman, and after forty genera-tions of cross-breeding, Redenbacher and Bowman came up with a variety of corn that, when popped, was lighter and fluffier than the standard store-bought variety. And by carefully maintaining an exact moisture level when slowly drying the corn, Redenbacher could be assured of an almost one hundred percent probability that each kernel would pop when heated to the right temperature.

Producing the popping corn was one thing. Marketing it was another matter altogether. Redenbacher spent four years driving through Indiana and Illinois searching for farmers willing to grow the corn and retailers willing to sell it. But farmers saw no future in his corn, as it yielded less per acre than most seed corns, and retailers balked at the price, pointing to the fact that there were scores of different popping corns already on the market.

By this time, Redenbacher had invested ten years in a product with nothing more to show for his effort than a handful of kernels that looked identical to virtually every other variety. But the eleventh year made all the difference.

That was the year that the Chicago marketing firm of Gerson, Howe, and Johnson suggested that Redenbacher put his photograph on the label and change the name from Red Bow to Orville Redenbacher's Gourmet Popping Corn. Redenbacher thought this advice absurd. Who would want to buy a jar of popcorn with the picture of a sixty-three-year-old man named Orville Redenbacher on the label? But he had tried almost everything else, so he did as the marketing firm recommended.

First, though, he tested the market by sending a case of his newly labeled corn to the manager of the gourmet food department at Marshall Field's in Chicago, the biggest retailer in the area, without either a note or a return address. A month later Redenbacher called the man and asked if he liked it. The manager not only liked it, he ordered a pickup truck full. And he asked Orville to be on hand to autograph jars as they sold!

Twenty years later, Orville Redenbacher's Gourmet Popping Corn is the world's leader in a market that sells in excess of one billion pounds of popping corn each year.

Asked about his philosophy of life, Redenbacher replied: "I've followed the classic homespun principles. Never say die. Never be satisfied. Be stubborn. And be persistent."

Perseverance in the case of Redenbacher was a good

thing. But it's a good idea to remember that this value, like so many of the others I discuss, is only good so long as it is applied to "doing what is right."

I think of perseverance as consistency under pressure. This is something that everyone can relate to since the pressure of modern life affects all of us. We all require perseverance just to get through the day. Financial pressures, layoffs, sick children, hectic schedules, isolation, and the resulting stress are just a few of life's many pressures. Perseverance gives a person the strength and resolve to accept whatever comes, to face life head-on, and to stand firm.

The power of perseverance is most evident in its versatility. Perseverance can manifest itself as steadfastness to a cause or ideal. It can mean being patient, like my father waiting for a heart transplant, or a farmer waiting for a crop to come in. It can mean paying attention to small details or adherence to a larger vision. When we persevere, we are able to reach the goals we set and to keep the commitments we make.

Perseverance can serve to overcome challenges. However, this does not mean we should be inflexible. If our approach isn't working, we need to reevaluate our goals, and if they are still worth pursuing, we should look for another way to achieve them. As a sailor, I like to think of it as changing our tack—the angle at which we set our sails to the wind.

Perseverance grows out of an inner confidence in ourselves and our abilities. A steadfast belief in ourselves and, by extension, our goals, makes us tenacious. To give in is to give up on ourselves and our dreams.

My faith plays a significant role in my ability to persevere. Because I believe God will not forsake me, it is easier for me to press on toward my goals. Often this means hanging on in the face of criticism and life's daily challenges. God never has and He never will give up on us.

As with initiative, people who persevere show self-discipline and courage. Rather than running away when difficulty strikes, they face the difficulty with dignity and strength. While rejection stops and even destroys some, people who persevere walk away from rejection more determined than ever.

Like initiative and work, perseverance has played an important role in the success of Amway. There were many instances in their early business endeavors when it would have been easier for Dad or Jay to throw in the towel. In the early 1940s they opened a flight school, only to be told that the runway they planned to use wouldn't be completed as scheduled. Since they already had students lined up, they decided to strap floats on the plane and start pilot training on the river next to the airport. Then there was the time when their sailboat, the *Elizabeth*, sank off the coast of Cuba, en route to an adventure in South America. Instead of coming home immediately, as most people expected, they continued their adventure by plane, tramp steamer, and riverboat. And when they started selling vitamins, before people had any awareness of the value of food supplements, people thought they were crazy. Then to go on to become soap salesmen? Who would ever want to do that? But they stuck with it, and their perseverance has rewarded not only them but millions of people who today benefit from Amway products or the Amway business opportunity.

Walt Disney went bankrupt several times and had a nervous breakdown before he finally met with success. Albert Einstein failed math. And Scottie Pippen, a guard for the

Chicago Bulls, was equipment manager for his high school basketball team before he actually played on the team. The talent in all of these individuals was there, but so was perseverance.

America's history is rich in perseverance. Without the endurance of the Pilgrims who settled this country or the tenacity of our founding fathers who fought for its freedom, our lives would be very different today. Our early settlers and pioneers suffered great hardships in crossing the Great Plains, in overcoming drought and disease, in clearing the land and building their homes and communities. Much of the work has been done for us, which is why, in many ways, I think we have lost some of the fighting spirit that made this country great.

While no one looks forward to adversity, it is often adversity that provides the catalyst that forces us to set worthy goals, to persevere in meeting them, and to reach our full potential. This is what Judy Petrucci, from Lyons, Illinois, learned.

Petrucci, a housewife and mother, was a very committed woman by nature, devoted to home and family. But she had never thought of "taking on city hall" until a small, but significant, incident took place. Early one evening, Petrucci mentioned to her seven-year-old daughter, Gina, that her great-aunt Mary had been an entertainer in her youth. To Petrucci's surprise, she discovered that Gina thought this meant that Auntie Mary had danced naked in front of men. Gina's automatic association forced Petrucci to open her eyes and acknowledge that the strip bars that had grown up in her neighborhood were making a very real and negative impression on her daughter. The truth was that their tiny community of Lyons, with its forty-three bars and five strip clubs, had degenerated into a moral cesspool.

Petrucci began to get involved in her local government, and she asked the city council and mayor to set sanctions against the clubs and bars. But what Petrucci had not counted on was the strength and tenacity of those who held a vested interest in maintaining the status quo. The "good old boys" were entrenched in city hall, neck-deep in kickbacks and bribes, and had no intention of letting anyone upset their applecart.

Petrucci appeared time and again before meetings of the town board of trustees, requesting action on what she considered glaring civic problems. She was rewarded for her efforts with contempt. When she attempted to speak at public meetings of the town board, she was denied permission and told that she had to have an appointment to speak. On several occasions she was even told that without a law degree, she couldn't know what she was talking about. Essentially, she was told to get lost.

But Petrucci wasn't about to go away. She was committed to making her hometown a decent place for her family, friends, and neighbors.

The comment about the law degree stung, however, and stuck with her. With the help of her husband, Fred, who took over most of the domestic responsibilities in their household, Petrucci returned to school. She attended college and then law school, and eventually passed the bar. Meanwhile, she ran for public office, over and over again.

Petrucci accumulated an impressive string of losses in the pursuit of civic office, running against some powerful politicos who were well entrenched. She was defeated in her bid for town trustee in three separate elections, and for mayor in one. As a matter of fact, she lost so many times that her daughter, Gina, now in her teens, began to question her mother's desire to continue. But Petrucci responded without hesitation. "When you believe in something, you just have to keep fighting for it."

Eventually, Petrucci's persistence paid off. She was elected to the town board as a trustee. Then, once she had access to the public records, she tore back the veil of secrecy that had been masking the underhanded dealings of local government for years. What she uncovered was staggering.

With an honest, reform-minded public official in place, the Federal Bureau of Investigation moved in, launching Operation Safebet and probing the allegations of corruption among city officials and others. This resulted in the indictment of seventy-six people.

In sworn testimony, the mayor and his cronies were accused time and again for their complicity in the degenerate commerce that had plagued Lyons. In the end, most of the bars and strip clubs were finally forced to close their doors forever.

Judy Petrucci decided to run for mayor one more time. With the trials as a backdrop, and preceded by her reputation as a crusader, Petrucci was elected with an overwhelming seventy-eight percent of the vote. In the same election, a reform slate was ushered in and took over the town board. Things kept changing for the better.

For starters, after having been denied her voice in local government for so long, Mayor Judy Petrucci opened the floor of all public meetings to all citizens interested in airing their views—no appointment necessary. And she saw to it that the agendas of the meetings were published in advance to encourage concerned citizens to take an active role in their local government.

Mayor Petrucci then cleaned house, firing the chief of police, fire chief, town attorney, town administrator, and building inspector. She also reclaimed over three hundred "special police" badges that the previous mayor had issued to his cohorts. Finally, she made personal visits to those still daring enough to risk running a bar or strip club within the borders of Mayor Petrucci's town. Throwing down the gauntlet, she informed them that her administration would not tolerate any more gambling, sales of liquor to minors, or prostitution.

The town of Lyons now boasts increased property values, and is attracting new businesses into those storefronts previously occupied by bars and strip shows. But there's another, less tangible asset that Judy Petrucci provided her town, and that is the feeling of civic pride. The citizens of that small community are proud of their town again, and they now have an opportunity to play a very real part in determining the quality of life for themselves and their families. Judy has more freedom for herself, and her fellow citizens have more freedom as well. And they have Judy Petrucci's perseverance to thank for it all. Because of her example, the town of Lyons understands the importance of persevering to "do what is right."

~~ 14 ~~

# Accountability

Accountability—taking responsibility for our own choices and actions—is a more relevant component to becoming free than we might first imagine.

While many things in the world around us are clearly out of our own control, we do have control over our own actions and reactions. In fact, unless we are willing and able to accept responsibility for our actions and our reactions, we will never be free.

When we do not take responsibility for our past actions, it is unlikely that we will take responsibility for our own future. We can make a commitment, take initiative, work hard, and persevere, but if through our actions we make the same mistakes, then we will never reach our goal.

Some like to blame others for what goes wrong in their lives, others blame God. When we hold ourselves accountable, we accept the blame for wrong choices. Accountability is part of my faith. I believe that we are all accountable to God for the choices we make. Thankfully, God is forgiving, but we must acknowledge our mistakes before Him.

Accountability depends on honesty and humility, as well as fairness and courage. This means simply recognizing and accepting responsibility for past mistakes and for the state in which we find ourselves.

Individuals can receive rewards for accomplishments and victories, but they are also held accountable for failures and defeats. Some societies are built around group responsibility, and power is viewed as coming from the group. The uniqueness of America is that it is built around individual freedom and personal responsibility.

Accountability is something we can learn ourselves, but it is also something that we have a responsibility to teach others. Mike Krzyzewski, the head basketball coach for Duke University's championship Blue Devils, learned this lesson early in life, and that, he says, made all the difference in his brilliant career in college basketball. Krzyzewski now teaches his players to be accountable by holding them accountable.

The son of an elevator operator and a cleaning woman, Krzyzewski grew up in the Polish north side of Chicago. As a teen he excelled in sports as well as academics, and he was awarded an appointment to West Point. One day during his first year there, Krzyzewski and his roommate were walking across campus when his roommate stepped into a puddle and splattered Krzyzewski's trousers and shoes. An upperclassman, standing a few feet away, immediately stopped Krzyzewski.

"What's the meaning of this?" he screamed in Krzyzewski's

face. "Don't you know the rules about wearing a clean uniform?"

As the older cadet ranted, Krzyzewski stood rigidly at attention, remembering the three answers allowed a plebe: "Yes sir!" "No sir!" and "No excuse sir."

None of these answers seemed appropriate. All sorts of excuses came to mind, but Krzyzewski had the good sense to respond as expected: "No excuse sir," he barked.

Although he initially balked at what seemed to be unfair treatment, in the hours and days to come, the more correct that response seemed to become for Krzyzewski. There was no excuse. He and his roommate should have watched where they were going. His shortcomings and failures were his own responsibility, no matter how great or how insignificant they were. Only by accepting that fact could he learn to accept them and therefore learn from them.

This insight made such an impact on Krzyzewski that he later based his "No excuses" coaching philosophy upon it. It is the same philosophy that has helped him win back-to-back national college championships.

For Krzyzewski, and the many players who have had an opportunity to play for him, accountability has benefits that go far beyond being on a winning team. Being accountable has helped them accomplish more and has improved their relations with teammates. It has led to a healthier attitude toward life, and a clearer conscience, which is essential to realizing true freedom.

Accepting responsibility and learning from our mistakes is essential. How we rectify them has a lot to do with how we feel about ourselves in the present and, ultimately, in our future direction.

Accountability requires restitution for mistakes. Restitution may be as simple as making a confession or an apology; but sometimes it requires more. A heartwarming example of this is the gesture a U.S. doctor made to the small English village of Polebrook.

Twenty-year-old Roger Johnson was a trained navigator, bombardier, and aerial gunman who had been assigned to a squadron of B-17 bombers—the legendary "Flying Fortresses" of World War II—and stationed at a camp near Polebrook. When returning to camp late one night, he missed the public transportation and found himself stranded in town. In order to make it back to camp in time for the next mission he had been assigned to and to avoid letting down his fellow crew members, he decided to borrow a bicycle that was leaning against the wall of an outbuilding. He made it back to camp on time, but when he returned from his mission and looked for the bicycle so he could return it, it had disappeared.

Johnson finished the war as a first lieutenant, returned to college, and subsequently graduated from medical school. He went on to become a successful trauma surgeon, and with his wife he helped establish the first hospital on a tiny island in the British West Indies. Then, at about the time most people start retiring, Johnson went on to law school, launching a second career as an attorney dedicated to helping fellow doctors deal with lawsuits.

Despite a forty-year career dedicated to the service of others, however, something still nagged at Johnson. It was that bicycle he had taken and never returned. He remembered all too well the anguish he himself had felt as a child when someone had stolen the bicycle that he had purchased on credit and that he used to earn a small but important income. His mother had made it a lesson in responsibility when she insisted he pay off the loan despite the fact that he no longer had the bike. He also remembered the kindness that the people of Polebrook had extended to him and his cohorts.

Thus, at age sixty-eight, Johnson decided it was high time to make amends. He ordered one hundred new bicycles from the Raleigh bicycle company in England and had them delivered to Polebrook. He then spent an afternoon on the same runway he used to take off from, handing out bicycles to children who needed them.

It would have been easy for Johnson to let himself off the hook—after all, the incident occurred during wartime, and he had been acting in the line of duty. Instead, he took the initiative and made a magnificent gesture to the city of Polebrook. By so doing, he set an example that is still talked about in England, and he exhibited the personal responsibility that is a hallmark of a man of integrity.

Another soldier who demonstrated a remarkable sense of accountability and made amends to a spectacular degree is Gene Spanos, a former police lieutenant from Rosemont, Illinois, who fought in the Vietnam War.

For Spanos, the years of his service in Vietnam were a distant memory kept alive only by a shoe box of medals on the floor of his closet. He had been a marine sergeant with the Eleventh Engineering Battalion, stationed in the jungles of the DMZ, the so-called demilitarized zone between North and South Vietnam. Nearly two decades had elapsed since his twelve-month tour of duty when he learned that the approximately seventy-five thousand land mines he and his battalion had laid in the DMZ were still armed and hidden in the Vietnamese countryside.

According to an article that Spanos read in the *Boston Globe*, the hundreds of thousands of mines, bombs, and other ordnance left active at war's end had become a deadly playground for Vietnamese children straying from their villages, digging for scrap metal to sell at local markets.

Upset by this news, Spanos contacted his former battalion commander, who confirmed that the story was true: for the sake of convenience, and to lessen the risk of more American casualties, the decision had been made not to remove or destroy the land mines. The Vietnam War, Spanos learned, was the first conflict in our history where the U.S. military had not gone back and removed their mines.

"I was completely shocked," Spanos says. "I felt like the war had started up for me all over again."

Spanos didn't know what to do. He couldn't help thinking of the Vietnamese children who might lose their lives because they walked off the beaten path to pick a flower or because they were attracted to a shiny piece of metal protruding from the earth. Spanos felt accountable because he personally had laid hundreds of mines in the DMZ, along the periphery of fire-support bases where artillery and helicopter pads were located. Never mind that Spanos was only carrying out orders, or that these very same minefields had helped to protect his life and the lives of his fellow countrymen. Never mind that he was not part of the decision-making process at the war's end. There was no escaping the fact that the actions he had taken were directly contributing to the death of innocent children. He had to do something about it.

His first task was to decide on a course of action. A dozen or more phone calls and a trip to Washington convinced Spanos that his time would not be well spent trying to organize concerned citizens to lobby the government into changing its policy. Even if he could amass a sizable following of like-minded citizens and organizations, it might take a decade before the first land mine was removed. And even if both sides agreed in principle, there would be endless negotiations before U.S. soldiers would be permitted to return to the DMZ, or before Congress would authorize spending millions on a program that would be supervised by a government with whom the United States had no formal diplomatic relations. Moreover, the issue of land mines paled in comparison to what most veterans' groups viewed as the central issue in United States and Vietnamese relations: the return of POWs and MIAs. But to Spanos, his concerns were primary: hundreds of children stood to lose their lives if something was not done immediately.

Spanos and five other veterans of the Eleventh Engineering Battalion—among them a farmer, a fireman, a janitor, and an electronics store manager—decided to launch a privately funded citizen-based initiative to remove the mines. With a donation from a businessman who agreed to underwrite their efforts, and support from a host of government agencies and military advisors, Spanos's group, calling themselves Vietnam Revisited, set about obtaining military manuals, technical data, and battalion maps that revealed the exact locations of the land mines. In a number of instances they had to reconstruct maps based on the memories of the soldiers whose responsibility it had been to plant the minefields. Spanos and his team then obtained permission from the Vietnamese government to visit the former DMZ and develop liaisons with local military and police officers whose job it would be to coordinate the removal of the mines.

"It was exciting to see how many people wanted to help," says Spanos. "I could have filled two planeloads with veterans willing to return to Vietnam to remove those mines."

Nearly two years after he had begun his effort, Spanos and his team landed in Hanoi. To their surprise, they were saluted at the airport by five former North Vietnamese Army (NVA) officers, eager to help them get acquainted with the new Vietnam. A few days later Spanos and his men were flown by Air Vietnam into Khe Sanh and other locations in the DMZ where Americans had seen some of the bloodiest fighting during the war.

"Coming in through the rolling clouds, there was the most beautiful and peaceful landscape that I had ever seen. It was like out of a painting or something. And then I got to thinking about those minefields."

Spanos and his men immediately made contact with the Vietnamese army commander of the former DMZ, and they began pinpointing the areas where they believed land mines had been planted. Just as he had suspected, an average of four out of five minefields were still intact. It was a special moment for Spanos to hand deliver their maps to the local militia, along with technical advice on how to dismantle the mines.

Among the many local villagers they met was Colonel Ho Minh Thanh, a former NVA colonel, who revealed to Spanos the problems of limited medical facilities, acute lack of medicine, and a large number of children with war injuries or deformities. This became an additional inspiration for the second trip Spanos made to the DMZ as he continued carrying out his long-term goal of removing the land mines. On this second trip he arranged for a special export license that permitted him to ship more than $200,000 worth of medicine into the country.

Among the many lives that Spanos has affected is that of six-year-old Nguyen Xuan Nghin, an armless child whom he brought back to the Shriners Hospital for Crippled Children in Chicago. Spanos proudly displays a recent photograph of Xuan, fitted with new "arms," riding through the streets of Ho Chi Minh City on an American-made mountain bike outfitted with training wheels.

Besides the pleasure Spanos took in making peace with himself and the children of Vietnam, there came an unforeseen bonus. That was seeing the country in an entirely new way.

"I just couldn't get over the change that had taken place in me as well as in the country. Vietnam had smelled like death the last time I was there. Now the country was beautiful. To see Vietnam in peacetime was the best thing that could have happened to any American who had seen it in wartime."

Like Roger Johnson, Gene Spanos could have legitimately argued that the actions he took during the war were justifiable because they were in the line of duty. Yet he took years out of his life to go back and make corrections, not just for himself, but for the entire country.

When we take responsibility and are accountable for our actions, we are doing what is right, and we are protecting freedom for ourselves and others.

## 15

# Cooperation

Earlier components of becoming free have addressed individual effort. Cooperation, or working together toward a common goal, requires the involvement of at least two people and very often more.

Depending solely on ourselves for everything we need would be both inefficient and ineffective. While it is necessary to become self-reliant, I don't mean to suggest that we do it without cooperating with others. While dependence is anathema to freedom, interdependence is not. In fact, interdependence can contribute to greater freedom for the individual and for society as a whole.

Just as we all have unique gifts, we also have different needs, working styles, and points of view. In order to be able to tap into the marvelous resources that others offer, we must find ways to work with these differences, harmoniously and productively. Each of us has individual goals and aspirations, but it is only through cooperation with others that we will be able to achieve them.

Almost everything we do requires us to be part of a team or a partnership, whether it is as a marriage partner, as a family member, as a co-worker, or as a student. Cooperation is the "grease," you might say, that makes these teams and partnerships work. Life in our busy cities and on our roadways requires cooperation. When we are negotiating a busy intersection, we must cooperate with one another to avoid a collision. At a four-way stop, we must cooperate with the other three drivers to get through the intersection without colliding. If we refuse to follow procedures and respect the rights of others, negotiating our way through the numerous interpersonal encounters we have each day will be difficult.

Almost everything we do requires cooperation. The better we are able to cooperate, the more we will accomplish. When we cooperate, we join our talents, skills, and enthusiasm to achieve the goals we set. Together, there is no limit to what we can accomplish.

The success of Amway illustrates this well. The growth of a small family business begun in the basements of two homes into a multibillion-dollar international corporation in the span of thirty years has required a great deal of cooperation. Initially, there was cooperation between the two founders and later the founding families. There has also been wonderful cooperation between company employees and our distributors. Today, there is also cooperation between Steve Van Andel, the son of my father's partner, and myself. While I am president of the Amway Corporation, Steve is the chairman, and together we form what we call the Office of Chief Executives. Our personalities and working styles are different from our fathers', so our cooperative efforts are also different, although still effective. The most important things that Steve and I have in common are our faith, love of family, respect for our parents, and our commitment to our employees, as well as to Amway distributors and customers. We have a huge responsibility, with more at stake than ever, so cooperation is as important as it has always been.

Ours is a business that is built entirely on trust, and we can't trust those who aren't cooperative. Distributors are not going to base their own livelihood on a company they can't trust. Just as Amway distributors have brought their entrepreneurial zeal and an interest in expanding their Amway business, company employees have brought technology, an environmental awareness, and a creative approach to product development. Others have ensured the reliable supply of products and bonus checks. Indeed, cooperation is the grease that has kept things running smoothly at Amway.

The spirit of cooperation is easily seen in our nation's pioneers, who fostered a culture that put a high premium on settlers helping settlers, and neighbors helping neighbors. People needed help harvesting and threshing their grain crops, raising the frames for new barns, surviving the ravages of blizzards, putting out fires, or helping when illness incapacitated them. They built towns and cities where people could live and work together, and constructed roadways and railways to connect them. The same spirit of cooperation must be practiced today.

The entire free-enterprise system is built on the strength of cooperation through human action. I can grow potatoes and you can grow corn and we cooperate so that we both get to eat corn *and* potatoes. This system allows people to specialize and do what they do best, each person's unique contributions combining to benefit the whole.

Cooperation not only sounds like a nice thing—it really works. When individuals cooperate, companies merge, or strategic partnerships are formed, they do so because they know their combined strengths will have a $1 + 1 = 11$ effect. This was noted in a 1982 *Saturday Evening Post* article describing the rapid growth of my father's and Jay Van Andel's partnership and business enterprise. When we cooperate, each of us is better off at the day's end. It allows us to achieve our goals in concert with others.

Unfortunately, as a result of living in a world where many of our needs are being met by large, impersonal organizations, many of us are less aware of the essential nature of cooperation. Children don't see or know many of the people who take care of their family's needs. They don't meet and form relationships with the people who generate the electricity for their homes, grow the food they eat, deliver the mail, or pick up the trash. Frequently, the type of cooperation we once had with community members, friends, and neighbors is now accomplished with relative strangers. The family-owned neighborhood market has given way to "food warehouses" with checkout lines that run as far as the eye can see.

In some respects, the impersonal nature of modern life calls for greater cooperative skills. With strangers, we don't have a relationship to rely upon, or a particular mode of communication already developed to help in the process.

Because of this, good communication skills are more necessary than ever before. It is not surprising that communication has come to be such an important element of life that people even get university degrees in communication studies. Like cooperation, communication requires a minimum of two people. There must be both a person sending information and one receiving it for communication to take place. Most of us have less difficulty with giving than we do with receiving communication. But we must do both if cooperation is to occur.

Many promising cooperative ventures are never fully realized because of poor communication or the failure to clearly articulate needs and expectations. Consider the story of the minister who asks his vestry to approve the purchase of a chandelier. But each time he raises the subject, the proposal is voted down. Frustrated, the minister asks the church clerk what the problem is. The clerk replies: "There are three reasons. First, I don't know how to spell it for the minutes. Second, there isn't anyone at the church who can play one of those things. And third, what we need around here are some new lights."

An inability or refusal to communicate and cooperate defeats the purpose of any team or partnership. When we act independently and don't cooperate with others, we are less likely to achieve our goals. By not cooperating we are unable to benefit from the strengths and talents of others, and are restricted by our own limitations.

A common misperception is that people have to be similar if they are to cooperate effectively. In my experience, the best partnerships are formed by those whose skills and talents are dissimilar, but complement, or complete, one another—as evidenced by my father and his partner, Jay Van

Andel. Their cooperative ventures began years before they started Amway, when the two of them were students looking for a way to get to and from high school. Jay, whose father was a car dealer, had the car; my father had a quarter a week for gas. Together, they met their goals. Their dream of owning a business together took shape during those car trips. When Jay's father hired them for a job, they found out that they liked working together. Each brought different skills to the partnership. Dad brought his ability to motivate people, and Jay brought his administrative and organizational skills.

But most importantly, Dad and Jay shared the same goals. As Dad has said, they had many different ideas, but the same ideal. I'm happy to say that it is the same for Steve and me. As Dad once said to a friend inquiring about the future of our family business, "Just because Jay and I got along does not necessarily mean the kids will. They will have to find that out for themselves." Because we were taught the value of cooperation, Steve and I work and cooperate extremely well together.

Having recognizable and common goals is essential for cooperation. In fact, one of the primary methods for fostering cooperation is to realize that we all have some things in common. We can see examples of this even with something as common as highway driving. Although drivers on the freeway do not necessarily have the same destination, they do share some goals—one, for instance, is safe travel.

There is a sense of communal purpose that causes groups of people to cooperate with each other. A story that nicely illustrates this spirit of cooperation recently took place in Ivanhoe, Virginia.

It started when Maxine "Mack" Waller began hearing stories from her mother-in-law about how beautiful and what fun her hometown of Ivanhoe had once been. There had been theaters, an opera house, and many fine restaurants before an economic downturn resulted in local businesses pulling out. First the manufacturing companies left, followed by the banks, lawyers, and doctors. Next went the theaters, restaurants, and drugstores. The town's population of 4,500 dropped to around 600.

One morning Mack stood on the main street of Ivanhoe and took a long, hard look at her town. She saw dingy, unpainted houses. A school with broken windows sat empty on a weedy lot. Children had to travel thirty miles to attend school, so many of them didn't bother; when they entered their teens, they just dropped out.

When Mack read in the newspaper that the county planned to sell off some of Ivanhoe's land to raise funds for investment in other, more prosperous towns, she decided it was time that she and her fellow townspeople got together and did something. "For so long I kept waiting for the government to take some action around here. Now I realized it was up to the people who lived here to do something about it."

Inspired by Mack's leadership, the residents of Ivanhoe worked together, planning a weeklong "celebration" that would mark the beginning of the rehabilitation of Ivanhoe. Volunteers sold space in a "human chain" they were planning for three dollars a place. People created teams that painted buildings, cleared empty lots, and generally cleaned up the town. At the end of that week, residents celebrated their joint efforts by joining hands in their symbolic chain, which went for two miles across their town. They called it Hands Across Ivanhoe.

The town used the money that was raised to successfully

lobby foundations for community-improvement grants. "Faith in the future has now replaced despair," Mack says. "By joining hands, Ivanhoe has pulled itself together."

As Mack points out, the result of cooperating and working together is not only the completion of a job, but the sense of accomplishment that comes from that cooperative effort. The advantage of teamwork is not only the practical aspect of completing a job; it's the right thing to do. People who cooperate and support each other live happier and healthier lives. We need to be connected. It's part of God's design. And to remain connected, in successful relationships, we must be cooperative.

The peace that comes with shalom could not possibly be accomplished without cooperation. This is not the enterprise of a lone ranger. Cooperation requires a great deal of humility, because when we think we are king of the roost, cooperation does not come easily. But if we, in America, recognize that we are to be "one nation under God," we can all swallow our pride, stand shoulder to shoulder, and work together.

The spirit of cooperation fosters friendships and bonds that are essential to surviving life's challenges. The history of the United States is filled with the spirit of cooperation. For the benefit of their families and communities, citizens reached out across religious and ethnic divides to coordinate their skills and resources to benefit, strengthen, and preserve our freedom. Despite the fact that our pioneers had a strong sense of individualism and self-reliance, they still came together and organized into wagon trains before venturing out into the Great Plains.

Joy and Danny Murray from Bostic, North Carolina, experienced this same kind of cooperation when fighting to save their dairy farm.

As with everyone else in rural Rutherford County, the drought was already taking its toll on the Murray family and their 110-acre farm. Vegetables in their garden were withering on the vine, and their one hundred Holstein milk cows were picking at stubble in the pasture.

Danny Murray, a second-generation dairyman, supplemented his income by driving a school bus and taking on side jobs with his backhoe and tractor. Joy had taken a part-time job in the school lunchroom. Now, with the barn empty, and no hay to be found within the state, they seemed to have no choice but to begin selling their livestock or see them starve.

Then things started to take a turn for the better. A good Samaritan, a farmer from another area, who had heard about their starving animals, drove up one day and emptied four bales of hay out of the back of his pickup truck, refusing to take payment. This act of compassion meant everything to the Murrays.

Not long afterward, the Murrays and other farmers got an excited call from Ed Biddix at the local Farm Extension Office telling them that several farmers from Kentucky had sent up some hay. Murray was thrilled but told Biddix that he would have to find some money. "Don't worry about it, son," Biddix said. "The people heard about our situation and they just want to help out. The hay's a gift."

As it turned out, the Kentucky farmers were themselves running low on hay, but they wanted to help anyway. They also sent words of encouragement in a letter that was found in the hay.

This contribution triggered an idea for Danny. Maybe he

could get hay from other areas where the drought had not hit. Again with the help of Ed Biddix, the Murrays were able to identify a source in Ohio. When Danny called the farmer, Alva Clarke, Alva said that he had two hundred bales he could give them. The only problem was getting the hay to Bostic. Ed then connected Danny with Doug Atchley at Atchley's Construction in town. Although Doug didn't think he had a truck going in that direction for weeks, he called back shortly to say that he had arranged for a delivery to Ohio for the next day. He was going to donate the use of his truck, and the driver, Junior Kiser, wanted to donate his time and effort too.

The next day, after hours of driving, Junior and Danny arrived at the farm in Ohio. They were greeted by Clarke, who joined Danny and Junior in the long, arduous task of loading the bales onto the back of the truck. Before they knew it, several of Alva Clarke's neighbors had come to help. Many hands make light work. Never had this saying been more true than that day in Ohio.

When they got to the two hundredth bale and Danny started to close up the truck, Clarke said, "You can't quit now. There's a lot more hay in the barn. . . . I'm not going to let you boys leave until you squeeze every bale you can onto that truck." They were able to load on a total of 430 bales. And when Danny and the truck driver finally got back to Bostic two days later, Doug Atchley and a dozen others were there to help unload.

Never before had Joy and Danny Murray felt such support—from friends and strangers alike. Without the help and cooperation of many, their farm might not have survived.

While this story is about cooperation, it is also about compassion and optimism, the first components of becoming free.

If we do what is right, our outlook on life and compassion for others will result in cooperation. When this happens, everyone is better able to reach their individual and shared goals, thus advancing the cause of freedom.

# ❦ 16 ❦

# Stewardship

In previous chapters I have addressed the role that making and fulfilling commitments plays in becoming free. The commitment to stewardship, the final component of becoming free, is fundamental to doing what is right.

Stewardship is making good use of time, resources, and God-given talents. In keeping with my Christian perspective, I define a steward as "one who is entrusted with the management of property, finances, or other affairs *not his own*." This understanding is very much in line with the notion that what we have is entrusted to us—not as owners, but as stewards. In my view, in order to be good stewards we must accept that everything belongs to God, whether it is our bodies, our homes, the money in our pockets, or the earth that sustains us. This is also true of our talents, our abilities, and the opportunities that we are given.

I believe it is important for us to take care of these gifts, treating them with respect, developing and using them to the best of our ability. Being stewards of these gifts is doing what is right. As the Apostle Peter instructs us: "Each one should use whatever gift he has received to serve others, faithfully administering God's grace in its various forms."

God is the creator of all that exists. We are to be caretakers, since we have been made in God's image. Men and women were given dominion over everything on earth. Therefore, as good stewards, we are responsible to care for, not abuse, God's creation.

We must take care of the resources at our disposal. We must be good stewards of our finances, being fiscally responsible. Stewardship requires properly utilizing our God-given talents and skills in doing what is right. If we are not good stewards of our relationships with each other, we can't have cooperation, which is essential to productive life as discussed in the previous chapter.

When we hear the word "stewardship," one of the first things that comes to mind is community involvement. We are all members of communities, which may be as small as a school, church, or village or as large as our states or our nation. Our involvement may be as simple as keeping ourselves informed on local issues and writing to a local congressman, or as significant as holding public office. Stewardship requires taking action and encouraging stewardship among others, thus making them accountable for their actions.

Getting involved in our community's civic and political life is an important aspect of both upholding freedom and becoming free. No matter what our outlook or position, our contribution matters. We must not only speak up for what we believe is right, we must take action to do what is right. Our leaders are elected to represent us. If they don't know what we think about issues and if they don't know how we want them to represent us as good stewards of our concerns, then we are willingly giving up our freedom.

There are other ways to get involved in our communities. Nonprofit and charitable organizations need the skills and talents of many individuals to provide good stewardship in the communities they serve.

Betsy and I feel very strongly that we have a responsibility to dedicate time and resources to efforts that strengthen our communities. Our commitment to stewardship has led us to become increasingly involved in a variety of issues, whether working with others to get an arena built in Grand Rapids, providing educational scholarships to needy children, sharing our financial resources with others who need help, or supporting candidates who we feel will do what is right for our county, state, and nation.

We believe getting involved is a necessary part of living in a democracy. After all, "Democracy is not a spectator sport." If we sit back and let someone else make decisions, we abdicate our stewardship responsibility.

The approach and attitude we take to stewardship of our communities will determine the impact of our efforts. This was the case in Viroqua, Wisconsin, a town of just under four thousand people located twenty miles east of the Mississippi River.

Viroqua was dealing with many of the same problems that face hundreds of other rural American towns in an era of shopping malls and freeways. Its downtown four-block-long business district, once a brightly lit and thriving mercantile center, had gone into a downward spiral, and most business owners believed it was beyond repair. Infrastructures were deteriorating and beginning to look shabby. The railroad station had closed. Upon graduation from high school, the best and brightest students left for cities and towns where there were more opportunities. The entire town, it seemed, was locked in a "loser" mentality.

What seemed like the last nail in the coffin came when a sign appeared in a corn field north of town announcing that a Wal-Mart store was coming soon. To most shopowners in the old business district, this meant bankruptcy.

But one business owner wasn't about to see Viroqua become a ghost town. She was Nancy Rhodes, the owner of a Victorian-style bed-and-breakfast. Rhodes was something of a newcomer to Viroqua, and had not yet developed the loser mentality. Before coming to Viroqua, she had spent fifteen years in Southern California, dreaming of making her home in a town where people knew and cared for one another. She knew Viroqua was that kind of place because as a child she had visited her grandmother there. Now, as one of the local business owners, she found herself at town meetings, trying to remind its residents of what a special place they had, and why they shouldn't let it go.

"I developed a reputation as a troublemaker," Rhodes says. "That came from going around trying to get people stirred up. I badgered and challenged them until I got their attention. Then I asked what it was about Viroqua they liked and what length they were willing to go to hold on to it."

Rhodes had begun to formulate a plan to save Viroqua when she heard about a "downtown coordinator" named Bert Stitt, who worked for the state of Wisconsin. It was his job,

Rhodes learned, to help towns like Viroqua. At first Stitt, who was planning to leave his post, was unwilling to take on another assignment. But Rhodes wouldn't take no for an answer. She hounded him until he agreed to meet with her and thirty-four other town leaders. Stitt told them exactly what he told all the other town groups who were looking to dump their problems in his lap: Viroqua would have to turn *itself* around. He could facilitate their strategic-planning discussions and they could apply to the state's new Main Street program, but the work and the money had to come from them.

Rhodes continued to push until her fellow business-people agreed to explore the possibilities of the group process work that Stitt offered. That fall, sixty-five community people attended an all-day planning session that resulted in the formation of six groups. Out of that process, the decision was made to apply for the National Trust for Historic Preservation's Main Street program, which had been newly acquired by the state of Wisconsin. Stitt alerted them, however, that to qualify for the program, they had to raise a total of $150,000 for a three-year revitalization campaign.

At first, no one thought that such a large amount of money could be raised in such a small town. In fact, one Chamber of Commerce representative exclaimed that they had trouble getting members to pay their dues toward a $17,000 per year budget. How did Stitt expect them to raise $50,000 per year for three years? But then, Duffy Hoffland, the local president of the State Bank, courageously volunteered to shoulder the task of raising the money for revitalization.

"That was the moment our town began its long journey back from being a loser to becoming a winner," Rhodes says.

Hoffland and his fund-raising committee, which included Nancy Rhodes, went to work. And to everyone's surprise, they raised $170,000 in pledges.

The next step was to qualify for the program. A team of business owners was chosen to pitch their case before a panel in Madison, the state capital. To draw attention to themselves they dressed in turn-of-the-century outfits. Rhodes wore an hourglass gown, and the men accompanying her dressed in cutaways and striped pants. The idea worked.

With the program in place, the downtown revitalization team hired Theresa Washburn to run their campaign. She was a veteran of the Peace Corps with a degree in environmental design.

Washburn's top priority was to improve the look of the town. Toward that end, she was able to help establish low-interest loans that resulted in the renovation of thirteen stores.

The town also replaced the original streetlights that had long since vanished from the business district. Decorative lights were then strung along the tops of buildings, giving the downtown district a more festive air.

Within three years, seven new businesses had opened in "Old Town," twenty-two jobs were created, and the four-block business district had been given a face-lift. But the real payoff, according to Rhodes and other business owners, is the new sense of optimism in the town.

Rhodes was so excited by the results of their efforts that she teamed up with Bert Stitt and Associates in Madison, Wisconsin.

Their partnership now consults with communities in downtown development.

"It feels as though you're on a winning team," she says. "Everyone has got that attitude of should-do and can-do."

Thanks to good stewards like Nancy Rhodes, Duffy Hoffland, Theresa Washburn, and no doubt many others, Viroqua has been physically revitalized, and its spirit of hope and optimism has also been renewed.

Caring for our communities, as did the citizens of Viroqua, is one form of stewardship. Another form involves taking care of the earth and our environment. We all have a role in caring for God's creation, whether it is picking up a piece of paper blowing about in the street or investigating ways to stop pollution and to clean up problems that have already occurred.

The tradition of caring for our environment is one for which Amway is well known. We have received several awards for our role in environmental stewardship. In fact, we are one of only two companies to have been given the prestigious UN Environment Programme Achievement Award.

The attitude I believe all of us must adopt is one the Boy Scouts of America have long endorsed: We should leave a place in better shape than we find it. This is what inspired John Beal to clean up Hamm Creek, and Gene Spanos to remove land mines in Vietnam. When we look back on our lives, I hope we can honestly say that we are leaving our world in better shape than we found it.

As businesspeople, employers, and employees, we are stewards of the companies we work for. Business managers are stewards whose responsibilities include leaving a legacy for future generations. One way of doing so is through nurturing and grooming the future leadership of an organization. Another is to make responsible decisions that have long-term positive effects for the company's products, employees, customers, and community. If our decision making is based only upon what happens during the next three months or the next year, our decisions probably will not be sound. Native Americans take a long-term view when they say, "Everything we think, do, and say should be good unto seven generations."

In the corporate world it is hard to know how to judge a company's success. It's a widely held view that the primary goal of publicly owned corporations is to make a profit for their shareholders. Profits are important and necessary to the survival and growth of any company, but they should not be the sole measuring stick of performance. The cost of our actions to society and to our communities must be as important a consideration as the costs the company bears directly. If we manage our enterprises only for financial gain, it is like playing tennis with our eye on the scoreboard instead of the ball. And that's not the way to win a game.

A large part of stewardship is also taking care of property. The reasons are obvious. What most of us have the most difficulty accepting is the fact that our job is simply never done. The moment we get through doing the dishes there are more to be done. The driveway that was swept last week already needs another sweep. Last week's meeting has led to another meeting this week. Even though we helped our youngster with her homework yesterday, there is more homework to do today. The process never ends. Just when we think we can sit down and take a break, we have to get up and start all over again.

Proper stewardship requires that we take care of our possessions. Just as with honesty, learning this lesson in childhood makes our lives as adults much easier. One family I know teaches this notion to their children by putting toys in storage when the children don't take care of them. The toys are brought back after a period of time, when the children are more prepared to care for them.

As the definition suggests, part of stewardship is using our possessions wisely. For those who have more financial resources, the temptation is in acquiring too many "things." However, it is foolish to invest in things we do not have the time and/or interest to use, in spite of the fact that they can be cared for. Good stewardship requires us to plan our acquisitions carefully.

Good stewardship also means caring for ourselves. This includes feeding our bodies nutritional foods, supplementing our diet when necessary, and getting enough sleep, exercise, and recreation. Like many others, I must work hard to find balance in my life, but I make it a priority because my well-being depends on it. Most of us eat too much, exercise too little, work too many long hours, and devote too little time to recreation. It is easier to recognize the value of work, but we often undervalue recreation. It is not surprising that this word means "to re-create," and is something we must take time to do if we wish to stay healthy and maintain a better perspective on life.

Many men, particularly of my father's generation, believe that they are self-indulgent or weak if they stop to take care of themselves. They must overcome this perception if they want to enjoy a healthier, longer life. The Bible says that our bodies are the "temples of the living God." There is no question in my mind that we must use our intelligence, time, and self-discipline to keep our bodies healthy and strong.

But there is more to keeping healthy than just our physical bodies. Our emotions also need care and attention. Men and women who have love, friendship, and companionship in their lives are happier, healthier, and live longer than those who don't have these bonds. And people who don't have healthy social bonds suffer far more from stress and anxiety, and tend to die younger.

Stewardship is also required for our minds. Benjamin Franklin, well known for his intelligence, wit, and inventiveness, encouraged people to study mathematics because it strengthens the ability to reason. He also saw chess not as idle amusement, but as an aid in acquiring valuable qualities such as foresight, circumspection, prudence, as well as perseverance. What we choose to think about also impacts our well-being and our accomplishments. Similarly, what we expose ourselves to daily affects our minds. We've all probably heard the phrase "Garbage in, garbage out." This holds true for adults as well as for children.

Our character requires stewardship. We determine our actions and responses. Developing a good, strong character does not happen automatically. It requires effort, work, and diligence for both ourselves and our children.

The last, but not least important, aspect of our personal stewardship is caring for our spirit or soul. While not everyone believes that the soul even exists, there are many people who do believe, yet still don't take proper care of it. Daily prayers, meditation, and a general sense of gratitude and thanks to

God go a long way toward this. I know that this approach has brought more good to our family than any amount of business savvy, ambition, or financial reward.

Stewardship involves proper use of our talents and abilities. I would take this a step further and say "using our talents and abilities *well* by doing what is right." An athlete who exemplifies this kind of stewardship is Jackie Joyner-Kersee. Nearly all of us can remember her Olympic triumph in Barcelona, Spain, when Jackie ran faster, threw farther, and jumped higher than any woman had ever done before, and in so doing became, according to Bruce Jenner, "the greatest athlete in the world."

Jackie's life began on Piggot Street in a ramshackle one-story home in the slums of East St. Louis. Fortunately for her, the Mayor Brown Community Center was right across the street from her home. Run by Pop Miles, a man who volunteered his own time to work with the children, the center was the place where Jackie and her friends spent all of their spare time. There was an indoor pool and a track as well as activities such as dance and music.

Jackie competed in her first track event at the community center at age nine. She finished last. At her next event, held several weeks later, she won a second, a third, and a fourth place. The next time she earned three second places. And not long after that, she came home with the proud announcement that she had won five first places. From that day on, Jackie never stopped winning.

She had learned that when she practiced and worked hard, she got better and better in track and field, both running and doing the long jump. Not only that, she found out that when she practiced and tried hard she did better in school too. If she didn't understand something, she would take the work home and figure it out for herself.

Pop Miles, who saw Olympic potential in Jackie, took her under his wing and taught her to master a variety of specialties. She trained for the pentathlon and won the National Junior Olympic Championship when she was fourteen. She then went on to win the same event every year throughout her high school career, becoming one of the finest athletes in the state. When Jackie graduated from high school, her hard work and commitment to her schoolwork had paid off. She graduated in the top ten percent of her class.

As a young UCLA student, Jackie became their star basketball forward. Under the coaching of Bob Kersee, her future husband, she qualified and competed for the Olympic team in Los Angeles in 1984. She came within .06 seconds of winning a gold medal. Four years later, at the Goodwill Games in Moscow, she broke the world record by two hundred points and became the first American woman in fifty years to hold a multievent world record and the first woman outside the Soviet bloc to do so in a decade. In Seoul, South Korea, in 1988, Joyner-Kersee won two Olympic gold medals, and took another gold medal in Barcelona in 1992.

Jackie attributes her amazing talents and success to her determination, which she believes she inherited from her mother. She also attributes it to her positive thinking. With the aid of "little books on faith," she purposefully blocks out negative thoughts. But when things don't turn out the way she wants them to, her motto is "Whatever comes, accept it."

It is clear that Jackie, whose grandmother insisted she be

named after Jacqueline Kennedy "because someday this girl is going to be first lady of something," was born with talent. With her own determination, hard work, and practice, and with the help of supportive parents, Pop Miles, a devoted brother, and her dedicated husband/coach, Jackie became "the greatest athlete in the world."

Jackie has been a great steward of her talents and opportunities. But she has also proved herself a steward of the fame and fortune that came with it. The adoration she earned could easily have gone to her head. Instead, her feet stayed rooted firmly on the ground, and she recognized the role her fame could play in the lives of many young women. "I remember where I came from and I keep that in mind. . . . If a young female sees the environment I grew up in and sees my dreams and my goals come true, she will realize her dreams and goals might also come true."

And Jackie is as much a leader off the field as on, contributing to the community she came from and being an important role model for many.

"I too can be a cheerleader," Joyner-Kersee says. On the heels of her success in Seoul, she founded the Jackie Joyner-Kersee Community Foundation in order to help young people in urban areas throughout the country realize their potential. A substantial portion of her endorsement earnings has gone to this foundation, and she has continued to fund its operating expenses. The foundation works with children at elementary, junior high, and high school levels, helping them to develop their abilities, not only through sports but also through academics, including communications and the arts. She has also co-authored a book, *A Woman's Place Is*

*Everywhere*, which has touched the lives of thousands of young people across the nation. Equally important have been her efforts to improve her childhood neighborhood in East St. Louis. She gave a scholarship to a National Merit Scholar from her old high school, and each year sends teams of children from her old neighborhood to the AAU Junior Olympic Championships. Last year, she invited one hundred children from St. Louis to join her in New York for the Thanksgiving Day parade. Now she is trying to get the Mayor Brown Community Center, the place she got her start, restored and reopened.

Jackie's athletic success brought many lucrative product endorsement offers and, subsequently, a substantial income. When it came to handling these finances, Jackie continued her tradition of stewardship, investing in many worthwhile causes.

As we can see, stewardship of our finances does not mean digging a hole and burying our money, as the one servant did in the parable of the talents. It means investing one's resources wisely so that they will bear fruit. The fruit could come in the form of greater knowledge, medicines to heal the sick, the creation of new jobs, improved products and services to enhance the quality of life, better schools to educate our children, or opportunities, hope, and inspiration.

We must all teach our children how to be financially responsible. While Betsy and I provide for our children's needs, we also give each of them a monthly allowance. The amount is determined by their age. With this money they can buy whatever it is they want beyond the necessities, as long as they exhibit good stewardship. They are required to do their own budgeting, although we have set certain guidelines for them. A percentage of the money must be put away into savings for the future, and another percentage must be set aside for tithing. The children themselves investigate and determine what causes they want to support, and as they reach an age when they can understand, they will begin to learn about investment options for their savings.

As I stated earlier, stewardship means wise investing, carefully choosing what we want to buy and maintain. While money has often been blamed for the ills of mankind, in truth, it is just a tool that has allowed mankind to move beyond an economy based on barter. It facilitates free trade, just as strings of beads or shells did for Native Americans. If we treat money with respect and keep its role in perspective, it should only help rather than hinder us.

While relationships do not fall into the category of material things, they nevertheless also require steward-ship on our part if we are to sustain them. Maintaining relationships with our spouses, children, parents, siblings, relatives, friends, co-workers, neighbors, and community members requires time, work, and effort. Honesty, reliability, fairness, and humility, along with communication, respect, and civility, are all needed to sustain healthy, happy, and successful relationships.

While our mutual emotional well-being depends upon these efforts, there are other practical benefits as well, such as those that result from cooperation and accountability. We are all called to love our neighbors as ourselves, which directly affects the nature of our relationships and has a significant effect on our personal freedom.

Whether we are stewards of our relationships, of our abilities, fame, and wealth, as in the case of Jackie Joyner-Kersee, or of our communities, as in the case of the townspeople of Viroqua, proper stewardship has an important role to play in the process of becoming free.

# PART III

# PRESERVING FREEDOM:
## Helping Others to
## Do the Same

There are tools that each of us can use to help ourselves and others develop the abilities both to uphold freedom and to become free. This is of crucial importance, because it is not until *all* of us are free that any *one* of us will be truly free.

When we act with integrity we are contributing to the overall freedom of the world in which we live. But a few people acting with integrity will not fully guarantee their own freedom, no matter how self-reliant they are or how great their ability to do what they want to do.

No matter how honest people themselves are, they still have to lock their door or risk being robbed. Parents can consistently do what is right and still have to escort their children to school. A traveler can respect fellow travelers and still be required to have his or her bags searched at the airport. No matter how responsible some citizens might be, they will still be required to pay a portion of their income in high insurance premiums and taxes. In other words, those who do what is right pay a high premium for those who choose not to be responsible and not to respect the rights of others.

If freedom is to prevail for all, integrity can't just be within an individual; it must also permeate society. The amount of freedom that a society can offer depends upon the overall level of integrity and accountability of all of its citizens, both personally and in conjunction with others.

This leads us to two inevitable conclusions. If the citizens of our society are to become whole and stand together, they need a common goal. If they decide, as our forefathers did, that the goal is freedom, then they must help each other develop integrity and self-reliance. There are powerful tools, in the form of personal qualities, that foster a commitment to upholding the rights given us by our Creator. I have chosen eight that I believe are most effective. They are encouragement, forgiveness, service, charity, leadership, opportunity, education, and brotherhood. Proper stewardship of these qualities will preserve freedom.

## ❧ 17 ❧

# Encouragement

Encouragement means holding others to high standards, recognizing their potential and not underestimating them. It can mean encouraging them, not just to become self-reliant and capable of achieving their goals, but to develop integrity and the character traits that accompany it. We not only can, but must, encourage others to be honest, fair, and reliable. Further, we must encourage them to exhibit self-discipline and to work hard, to be accountable, and to persevere at what they do in order to achieve their fullest potential.

There has been a lot of talk recently about teaching self-esteem. I don't believe it can be taught, but it can be nurtured through encouragement. In order to be effective, encouragement must be based in reality. We can't simply tell people they are capable. When there is no basis for it, encouragement rings hollow to everyone, especially the recipient. We must encourage the best traits in others and offer help and support in areas where they struggle.

Sometimes the focus of our encouragement is just a tiny gleam we see shining in someone's eye. When I was in high school, my football coach took me aside and told me he was going to start me as a quarterback. He said, "You might not be as big or as strong as the other guys, but you have field leadership that the team respects." That coach saw something in me that I hadn't seen myself, and his encouragement and faith in me gave me confidence. You can be sure I worked hard to live up to his analysis, and to this day his comment encourages me to reach my full potential.

All children, psychologists say, are born with a drive to become competent. This becomes evident the moment an infant first attempts to hold up its head, and remains apparent as the child strives to develop greater abilities and become more and more self-reliant. It follows then that encouraging competence in others will have a positive impact on their abilities. Recent studies indicate that the boost that comes from encouragement is not only psychological but physiological. The positive reinforcement that comes from receiving encouragement actually stimulates neurotransmitters in the brain, enhancing energy levels, creativity, and endurance.

Professional sports coaches have known this for years. To encourage—literally, to "give courage"—is one of the most potent tools at a coach's disposal. That's why coaches are constantly searching for new and innovative means of encouraging their players. It's also why the best coaches are both skilled physical trainers and amateur psychologists, dedicated to the art of motivation. Even someone with mediocre talent can become great in the hands of the right coach.

Reggie Jackson, the gifted baseball player, summed this up when he described what makes a coach great: "He has a knack for making ballplayers think they are better than they think they are. He forces you to have a good opinion of yourself. He lets you know he believes in you. He makes you get more out of yourself. And once you learn how good you really are, you never settle for playing anything less than your very best."

Another athlete who appreciates the power of encouragement is Kristi Yamaguchi, whom I had the pleasure of meeting at the opening celebration of our new arena in Grand Rapids. She is one of the most prominent and recognizable of today's American figure-skating stars. Her gold medal performance in the Albertville Winter Olympics vaulted her into international prominence. Fans took her success as inevitable, but success in a sport so physically demanding was not always assured for Yamaguchi. As a matter of fact, it was a long shot.

At Kristi's birth, in Hayward, California, medical specialists identified serious problems with her feet and legs—a congenital deformation known as clubfoot. She was put into corrective casts for the early part of her childhood; and later, to promote strength in her legs, she was put through an aggressive regimen of exercise, dance, and ice-skating classes.

Wearing corrective casts can be painful, as it stretches the tendons and ligaments in an effort to re-form the misshapen foot. Unfortunately, these corrective casts can also cause embarrassment to the wearer, especially around other children who don't have to wear them. And the seemingly endless rounds of exercise classes can be exhausting. It would be easy for someone to just give up when facing such compound challenges.

But time and again, whenever her resolve faltered, Kristi received intense encouragement from those around her. First, and most importantly, Kristi's parents were there for her, encouraging her to keep at it, no matter what. Enveloped and supported by their love and positive attitude, she thrived, eventually conquering the physical disability that threatened to limit her life.

Kristi's formal training in skating began at age ten, under coach Christy Kjarlsgard Ness. Like Kristi's parents, Ness gave endless encouragement and boundless support throughout Kristi's training. Kristi's closeness to and confidence in her coach strengthened the impact of that encouragement. But skating for therapeutic purposes was not enough for Kristi. After mastering the basics, she paired with Rudi Galindo and began the serious training required to become proficient in this demanding sport.

Eventually, she began competing, and, with Galindo as a partner, first tasted real success when they won the junior pairs title at the U.S. Figure Skating Championship. From then on it was a string of successes. Kristi won the singles title, and again, with Galindo, a pairs title at the World Junior Skating Championship. Returning to the U.S. Figure Skating Championship, Yamaguchi and Galindo again won the pairs title and Kristi placed second in the singles. Now it was the cheers of the fans that encouraged her to greater heights.

From then on until her breathtaking gold medal performance at the Olympics in Albertville, France, Kristi concentrated on perfecting her unique singles style, notable for its physical difficulty and its complexity. That same year, she won both the World and U.S. Figure Skating titles, assuring her a place among such current luminaries of professional figure skating as Scott Hamilton and Katarina Witt.

Kristi has not forgotten the tremendous gift of love and encouragement she received from her parents, her teachers, and the coaches and trainers who contributed to making her life a dream come true. The high standards they set and helped her reach strengthened her own commitment to encourage others by supporting several programs, notably the Make-A-Wish Foundation, whose mandate is to grant special wishes to children who have a terminal illness. Enhancing the lives of children who face challenges, as she did in her childhood, is an important part of her character. Her words of wisdom have encouraged many: "Make the most out of absolutely everything, and never stop believing in yourself."

My courage comes from my faith in God, and I believe that the more I can do to help others develop greater faith, the more I am "encouraging" them. Of course, encouragement can be expressed in a myriad of other ways, including a pat on the back, a hug, a bouquet of flowers, a family cheering section in the bleachers, or simply paying attention to someone. In business, a kind note, a phone call, a public word of praise, a thank-you, and, perhaps most important, recognition, are all ways to encourage others.

At Amway, we do a lot of encouraging. We give people pins, plaques, applause, and bonus checks. Sometimes there is so much cheering going on that people wonder if we are running business meetings or sporting events. But we believe this kind of encouragement is truly important. In fact, a great deal of our company's success can be attributed to the enormous amount of encouragement my father gave and still gives to our employees and distributors. He often says that he has spent his life being a cheerleader. I personally have been a beneficiary of this. Dad has always given me the best encouragement in the world and still does. No matter how difficult it might have been for him to relinquish the reins when he retired, he has offered me nothing but encouragement.

Sometimes encouragement just means being there for someone when we know it's important to them. Encouragement can't always fix things. For example, when we go to a funeral, we can't make the pain go away for the bereaved. But sometimes we have courage to spare, and out of that, we can give courage to others in their time of need. When we remember that courage comes from the heart, encouragement in difficult times is like taking a part of our own heart and using it to hearten others.

Encouragement is not nagging or being negative. It's not about penalties, control, or manipulation. Nor does it compare performances. Encouragement focuses on individual accomplishments. And encouragement always focuses on strengths, not weaknesses.

Sometimes we can discourage others and not realize it. While I still feel proud that my football coach saw potential in me, I am also angry when I remember being accused of cheating on a test in high school. Perhaps I was not the best student in the world, but I didn't cheat. So it was very discouraging to be accused of doing something I took pride in not doing. An unwarranted lack of faith in others can discourage them in the most insidious ways. People are far more likely to give up when they feel they can't win no matter what they do.

We can encourage others and show faith in them by

releasing control, when appropriate. When we step back and let others begin to take responsibility for themselves, we are, in essence, telling them that we know they can do it. And when we allow others more responsibility, we are encouraging them to become increasingly self-reliant and capable.

As parents and teachers know, encouraging children is a boost to the adult as well as the child. Not only does the adult have the satisfaction of seeing the child energized by his or her praise, but that energy radiates off the child and back to the adult. And when the child is successful, the energy is multiplied. It's like the old saying, "When we help someone up a hill, we are that much nearer the top ourselves." Encouragement can be infectious. Like laughter, it can spread from one to many.

For Thomas Monaghan, the founder of Domino's Pizza, encouragement was a key factor to his outstanding success. He has never failed to pay tribute to the very special person in his life who encouraged him to be anything he wanted to be and taught him that opportunity was everywhere. And Monaghan, even at an early age, had big dreams about what he wanted to be—a professional ballplayer, a priest, and an architect. His dreams, however, seemed impossible, for his father had died when he was nine years old and his mother's financial problems compelled her to put him and his brother Jim in St. Joseph's Orphanage in Jackson, Michigan.

Monaghan lived at the orphanage for the next six years. While he was there, he met the person who took his grand dreams seriously and encouraged him to pursue them. Her name was Sister Mary Berarda. And she knew that encouragement was the oldest and best form of therapy.

"Have faith in God, and have faith in yourself," Sister

Berarda kept telling him. "Then go out and do it. You can be anything you want to be."

Monaghan knew that she would support any of the goals he had set for himself, but the career that she was rooting for was as shortstop for the Detroit Tigers, her favorite team.

Sister Berarda supported and encouraged Monaghan in every way she could. She came to every baseball game he played and never scolded him when he skipped a meal to have an extra hour of practice.

Sister Berarda also read him books and stories about famous people. By teaching him about people like Henry Ford, Stanley Marcus of Neiman Marcus, and Ray Kroc, the founder of McDonald's, she was showing Monaghan that it didn't matter where we come from or how little we have to start with.

While in his youth, Monaghan became a first-class baseball player, but his entrepreneurial spirit had already begun to emerge. He started college twice with the idea of becoming an architect, and he might have finished if he hadn't run out of money. He then spent four years in the Marine Corps. When back in civilian life, he enrolled in the University of Michigan, and while he pursued his degree, he worked selling newspapers at a newsstand. Before long, Monaghan was in the position to buy the newsstand for himself *and* hire a team of newsboys to work for him.

Monaghan was in the midst of expanding his newsstand operation when he got a call from his brother Jim, who had become a mailman. Jim had a chance to buy a pizza parlor called Dominick's in Ypsilanti, Michigan, and wanted Monaghan to help him run it.

His original idea was to operate the pizza parlor part-time

at night, so that he and Jim could keep their full-time day jobs. But things didn't turn out that way. Soon after taking over the parlor they found themselves working full-time hours at both jobs. Jim eventually quit because he couldn't keep up with both jobs, and he believed his future at the post office was more secure. But Monaghan dropped out of school, sold his newsstand, and took the pizza parlor on full-time.

Under his management, the parlor went from a five-hundred-dollar-a-month loss to a profit. Soon he was able to expand to a second location, which also turned a profit. He wanted to expand the business at his second parlor, but there was a problem: not enough room to install more tables and chairs. His solution was to develop a take-out business.

This meant Monaghan was going to have to improve his services. The first thing he did was speed up the delivery time. Instead of the normal forty-five minutes, he got the time down to thirty minutes or less, guaranteed. He also bought a portable oven that kept the pizzas hot en route to their destination. Although now an industry standard, at the time use of such an oven was unique in the pizza business. Next, Monaghan introduced a vertical cutter-mixer for his dough. This too became industry standard. By the time he had introduced the radical concept of using corrugated boxes to eliminate crushed pizzas, his business had doubled and then tripled.

Monaghan went on to open a third store. Two years later he added six more. It wasn't long before he had sixty stores, and then a hundred. Along the way he changed his company's name from Dominick's to Domino's Pizza. Now Domino's is in forty-five countries.

Though a millionaire many times over, Monaghan has

never forgotten Sister Berarda's message: to have faith in God and faith in himself.

And he did realize another one of his dreams. He joined the Detroit Tigers—not as a player, but as the owner.

We can encourage others in many different ways. We can help them to develop integrity, to do what is right, to become self-reliant; and, as Sister Berarda did for Tom Monghan, we can help them to realize their dreams by supporting their confidence to go out and do what they want to do because it is right.

## ❦ 18 ❦

# Forgiveness

Forgiveness grows out of the recognition that failure is a part of life and is to be expected. We all fail at times. We all make mistakes. And we all need forgiveness.

It is easier to be encouraging when we accept imperfections in ourselves and others. After all, no one is perfect. When we forgive, we grant pardon without harboring resentment, or as the expression goes, "forgive and forget."

Forgiveness sends a powerful message of trust. When we show trust in people, they are more likely to live up to that trust. And when we forgive others, we also provide a good example for them to follow.

Forgiveness is vitally important to me because it is an essential part of my faith. Those of us who believe we have been forgiven through the sacrifice of Jesus Christ must also forgive others. God forgives our faults, and so should we forgive the faults of others. God instructs us to forgive. This is not only the right thing to do, it is "graciously Christlike." It is the essence of Christianity.

Forgiveness, like any other God-given virtue, is also practical. It can motivate and encourage growth. Parents, educators, managers, and leaders can empower their charges and breed initiative when they forgive mistakes that are made. The innovation and risk-taking so essential to progress and achievement depend upon forgiveness.

Tom Watson of IBM understands this principle. He once called into his office a member of his staff who had overseen a project that had ended up costing the company millions of dollars. The staff member, thinking he was going to be fired, decided to cut short the process by handing in his resignation. Tom refused to accept it. He couldn't possibly let the man go, he said; he had just spent millions of dollars training him!

Forgiveness is also essential to a good partnership and the healthy progress of a company. My father believes the key element in the success of his partnership with Jay was that they never said, "I told you so," to one another. Both partners always assumed the other was doing his best and had the best of intentions. When mistakes occurred, they focused on finding a solution and not on laying the blame. Forgiveness was always a given.

Betsy and I have an agreement, which we have violated only a very few times, that we never go to sleep at night angry with each other. This means that one of us has to apologize and the other forgive. Usually the problem, whatever it is, gets worked out sometime before dawn. Sometimes we don't get much sleep, but our relationship is stronger for it.

We also try to model forgiveness for our children. We make it clear that we are unhappy when they are disobedient, and we punish them or have them make up for their mistakes. But we don't hold grudges. Instead, we hug them and look for opportunities to give them some encouragement. And since forgiveness can be revealed only through our actions, we also let our children have a second and a third chance to prove that they have learned from their mistakes.

A man who might never have made anything of his life, if he had not experienced ongoing forgiveness, is Ron Dennis, a former soldier who served under General Gus Pagonis in Desert Storm.

Dennis started out in life as an abandoned child. Between jail and foster homes in Atlanta, Georgia, he lived on the streets, sometimes running with gangs, and sometimes just traveling alone. At times he stole food from supermarkets and clothes from wherever he could find them. As a boy he was picked up by the police more than fifty times. Then, at the age of eleven, while attending reform school, he heard about Boys Town, a boarding school in Nebraska, where the students themselves apparently made the rules. He begged his social worker to put him on the waiting list. Twelve months later he was accepted.

Dennis arrived in Omaha and was met by Jim and Sherri Gehman, who became his new "parents" at Boys Town. Discovering that he, a black child, would have white parents was quite a shock. An even greater shock was learning that he now had eight brothers. They would all be living together under the same roof—not because the government assigned them to this home, but because each child, like himself, had chosen to live at Boys Town. They were free to leave when they wanted to.

That first day on campus Dennis was stunned to see a banner that his new family had stretched across the big two-story brick house that would be his new home. It read: "Welcome Home, Ron!"

Soon after his arrival, Dennis was taken to see a statue of a boy carrying a smaller boy on his back. The inscription on the statue read, "He ain't heavy, Father . . . he's m'brother." At the time, the inscription seemed meaningless to Dennis, but eventually he came to understand its profound meaning.

That first night at Boys Town, Dennis's new family explained his responsibilities, which included participating in household chores. Later that night he was caught stealing food from the kitchen cabinet and was immediately confronted by his brothers. They told him that if it happened again, they would have to report him. Angry, Dennis climbed out of a window and ran away. But there was no car or abandoned building to sleep in as there had been on the streets of Atlanta. A few hours later—shivering and cold—he returned to his new home, where an older brother let him in.

Dennis ran away more than a hundred times over the next two years. Each time, his parents and older brothers were always there to receive him back.

On one occasion he vandalized the property of the Hugunins, another Boys Town family. Some of his friends didn't like them and Dennis took it upon himself to let them know by throwing paint all over the Hugunins' house and patio. That summer, he spent three hot months scraping white paint off brick. He was amazed that Bruce Hugunin came out every few hours, offering him lemonade and urging him to rest.

When the Gehmans, his adopted family, had to leave Boys Town, Dennis was convinced that he was going to be abandoned again. He couldn't imagine that anyone would choose him to move into their family. He almost fell over when he discovered that the Hugunins had requested that Dennis come to live with them. "I was overwhelmed," Dennis said. "Here were people who loved and cared for me no matter who I was and what I had done." Dennis vowed then that he would do everything in his power to live up to the trust they had shown in him.

Dennis eventually graduated from school, left Boys Town, and joined the marines. His family, however, was never far away. While serving in Kuwait during Desert Storm, he received hundreds of letters and cards from his brothers and sisters back at Boys Town. And when he returned to see Father Peter, the head of Boys Town, at the war's end, a dark blue banner with bold white letters was hanging outside his house. It read: "Welcome Home, Ron!"

No one who knew Dennis was surprised when he eventually became a teacher and started his own family at Boys Town, helping others as he had been helped. Forgiveness had transformed his life, and he was determined to transform the lives of others in return.

As Dennis tries to teach his students, forgiveness is not the same as condoning our own mistakes or those of others. It doesn't mean giving the stamp of approval to transgressions. It does no good to pretend something wrong didn't happen. It also does not mean that we shouldn't get angry when someone hurts us, or that we shouldn't let him know how angry we are. Nor is forgiveness evidence of moral weakness, as some claim. On the contrary, it takes greater courage to forgive than to hold a grudge. A contemporary theologian has gone so far as to say that we have an obligation to forgive those who have wronged us, and it remains an outstanding "debt" until we do.

Forgiveness does not mean that we allow ourselves to be doormats or put up with abuse. We must sacrifice only our resentment. Forgiveness also does not mean that we won't hold others accountable. We must honor others' choices and not shield them from the consequences of their actions if we want them to become self-reliant and to develop integrity. But holding someone accountable should never turn into revenge.

Forgiveness is necessary if people are to lead peaceful and productive lives. Harboring resentment or seeking revenge ultimately only creates more injustice. A woman who learned this firsthand was the late Vera McCoy, from McAlester, Oklahoma.

Many people knew McCoy as one of President Bush's thousand points of light—the woman who was invited to be her state's representative to the White House in recognition of the sixty years she served as a volunteer at the Oklahoma State Prison on the outskirts of her town. Few people, however, know of McCoy's personal struggle to forgive the inmate who had killed her son.

McCoy was at a prayer meeting at the First Baptist Church in McAlester when she learned that her thirty-eight-year-old son, Mark, had been shot. At the hospital, a nurse broke the tragic news. Mark was dead.

The sudden loss of Mark was especially difficult for

McCoy. She and Mark had become unusually close since McCoy's husband had died of cancer and her only other son had died from muscular dystrophy. Three months earlier Mark had moved in with McCoy with his two young children, in the wake of a separation from his wife, Wendy. Except for a daughter, who lived in Odessa, Texas, McCoy was now alone.

Mark's alleged killer was his own father-in-law. According to the police, Mark had been called to his house to intervene in a dispute between Wendy and her father, Charles. When Mark arrived, an argument flared up between the two men, and Charles shot Mark.

Vera McCoy sat in the front row at Charles's trial. The big white-haired man wept as he testified that he had shot Mark in self-defense. They had quarreled in the past, and he believed that Mark had come to harm him.

Charles was found guilty of second-degree murder and sentenced to ten years in prison—the same prison in which McCoy spent so much of her time teaching inmates how to read. A co-worker, Fay Durant, suggested that she volunteer at a different prison.

"I just couldn't do that," McCoy said. "There are too many people counting on me."

Twice a week McCoy forced herself to return to the Oklahoma State Prison, never seeing Charles, but knowing that the inevitable moment would come when they would cross paths. Her loathing for him increased with time because he had made no effort to apologize or to ask for her forgiveness.

Then a strange thing happened. Atop a pile of old newspapers on the kitchen counter, McCoy found a crossword puzzle that her son must have completed before his death.

That night McCoy went to sleep thinking about her

son and the crossword puzzle. Life had been a puzzle that he had been unable to complete. Then McCoy realized that she had yet to complete her own puzzle: she hadn't made peace with Charles. Preoccupied with her own hurt and sadness, she had been incapable of forgiveness and unable to see Charles as a weak and frightened man.

"I made up my mind not to hate because I knew that it would destroy me," McCoy told her neighbor. "I had to get on with my life. I had to learn to love Charles."

McCoy did just that. Then one night she invited him to join her in the prison chapel.

The silver-haired man she met there had aged considerably since she had last seen him. He was thinner and his shoulders were stooped. McCoy held back the images that raced through her mind: her son, the funeral, two fatherless boys. She approached Charles and hugged him.

"I want you to know that I have forgiven you," she said. "Understand that this does not take away my grief over what has happened. Nothing can do that. But I can forgive you."

As a Sunday-school teacher, prison mentor, mother, and grandmother, McCoy had always taught that merely saying you forgive someone isn't enough. There has to be a sincere demonstration of that forgiveness. McCoy's opportunity to demonstrate forgiveness came two years later. Charles was eligible for parole, and McCoy wrote a letter to the parole board supporting his release.

After being awarded parole, Charles became like a son to McCoy. He first brought her firewood, and then food and supplies when McCoy was housebound with pneumonia. Finally he sent her an invitation to join him and her grandchildren for Thanksgiving dinner.

It took all of McCoy's courage and strength to mount the steps to Charles's house and walk in through the screen door where her son had been shot. But she was glad she did.

"The shot that shattered my son's life could have shattered my own as well, and left me with a life of lonely bitterness," she later wrote. "But now I too was free."

McCoy learned that forgiveness benefits not only the forgiven but the forgiver as well. Forgiving does not require admission of guilt by the wrongdoer. Forgiving is a process and decision that requires no one's participation except the one doing the forgiving. Studies have shown that when longtime grudges are given up, blood pressure drops, and people become less anxious and generally psychologically more healthy. Researchers have observed self-confidence go up, depression go down, and more hopefulness and optimism toward the future.

In contrast, the unwillingness to forgive is known to have a negative effect on the emotional well-being, not only of those who fail to forgive, but of their offspring and future generations. When individuals are unwilling to forgive, they can become obsessed, pouring energy into anger and thoughts of revenge, mentally replaying the offense over and over. Some people become unable to focus on important matters, such as earning a living or taking proper care of their children. This kind of dysfunctional behavior then becomes part of the family's "system." And whether or not they acknowledge the behavior, it has a serious impact on the psychological health of their children. Forgiveness can break that pattern.

Just as it's important to forgive others, it's equally important to forgive ourselves. In fact, there is increasing evidence that forgiveness of our own imperfections and mistakes is essential to our own well-being and our ability to maintain relationships with others.

As Vera McCoy discovered, forgiveness is essential to freedom. While much of what happens to us seems beyond our control, we can control our reactions to what happens. Reacting with forgiveness frees us, and it also fosters freedom in others.

# ⚜ 19 ⚜

# Service

A s Mother Teresa has stated, "the fruit of love is service." I could not agree more. To me, service is also the giving of time, energy, and talent in accomplishing something for another. It provides us with a powerful vehicle to help others develop integrity, self-reliance, and the ability to live out their dreams. It is a wonderful outlet for us to act on our compassion, and it gives us opportunities to better see things through the eyes of others or to walk in their shoes.

When we serve others, we put ourselves into the position of mentor and helpmate. Depending on the type of service we provide, there are a myriad of other ways to positively influence and serve others. If we help children learn to read, we contribute directly to their self-reliance. If we work with a church youth group, we encourage spiritual development. Sitting on the board of directors of an organization can give us the opportunity to influence programs and policies that support self-reliance instead of dependence.

While this chapter is mostly about voluntary service, let's not lose sight of the fact that every moment in a day, whether on the job or on our own time, there are opportunities to serve others simply by giving them our best and going the extra mile to serve them in whatever we are doing.

As we learned from Lorinda Tucker in chapter 2, going the extra mile is a component not only of reliability but of service as well. There are also many small ways we can serve others, such as opening the door for someone who is struggling with groceries or letting people cut in front of us when they need to make a lane change in heavy traffic. We can serve others with as small a gesture as giving an encouraging word when someone seems to be having a bad day. Serving in this manner sets the tone for the rest of the day, for ourselves and for those we serve.

There are many opportunities in our country for more formally serving others. Indeed, volunteerism is an American tradition that goes back to the early years of our nation. Our public institutions such as hospitals and schools were built by volunteers. Citizens did not look to the government to provide everything for them. Alexis de Tocqueville asserted that America's desire and commitment to voluntarily serve others was one of the fundamental things that made our nation special. And that is still true today. Upwards of eighty-nine million Americans donate an average of 4.7 hours a week to groups and organizations that provide services ranging from legal aid and tax advice to flood relief. No other nation on earth even comes close to matching those figures. But our work is not finished.

If we are to foster integrity, self-reliance, and abilities in all of our citizens, and at the same time keep the necessity of governmental intervention to a minimum, each of us must serve in some capacity. The importance of this cannot be overstated. Today, there are many schools, agencies, and programs still in need of volunteers to support them with time, talents, and expertise.

There is a tradition of community service in the DeVos and Van Andel families and in Betsy's family too. Over the years, I have volunteered in many different capacities, everything from leading a Boy Scout troop to giving blood. At the moment I volunteer on several boards, including a university, a college, a hospital foundation, and a commission for the state of Michigan.

At Amway, the idea of service to our community and to our nation is an important part of our way of doing business. We want to give something back to our communities and to our country, which have given us so much. We urge employees and distributors to give a portion of their time and energy to such activities as improving their communities or helping in emergency relief efforts. This policy is supported by available leave time for Amway employees as well as by direct donations of products, tools, trucks, airplanes, and whatever else a situation calls for. But Amway is by no means the only corporation to take on civic responsibilities in this way. Each year a growing number of companies establish volunteer programs that support employee and corporate efforts to serve their communities. The Atlanta-based Equifax Company, for example, arranges for retiring employees to volunteer full-time while still earning a paycheck. Johnson and Higgins, a major insurance broker, shut down all of its

120 offices around the world for a day so that its 8,500 employees could do volunteer work for children. And Allstate Insurance has a philanthropic arm that focuses on neighborhood revitalization and safety. These are but a few examples of corporations encouraging service.

The desire of people to serve their neighbors is evidenced daily across our nation. In Langdon, New Hampshire, 450 residents fought bitter cold winds to rebuild a high school's agriculture building. Families in Cherry Tree, Oklahoma, held an old-fashioned barn raising to construct a recreational facility for youth. In Santa Fe, New Mexico, volunteers formed the Food Brigade to assist hungry neighbors and residents. In the aftermath of Hurricane Hugo, a pair of chefs from one of Boca Raton's most exclusive resorts closed their kitchens and reopened them in a parking lot to feed hundreds of refugees. Before the dust from the bombing in Oklahoma City had settled, thousands of people were headed into the city in vans, trucks, and cars to do what they could to help.

In all of these cases, individuals went beyond what was expected of them, simply because it was the right thing to do.

Linda Stillman personifies this spirit. For as long as she can remember, she had been interested in helping the blind. While raising her children, she took it upon herself to study braille. At the Helen Keller National Center for Deaf-Blind Youth and Adults in Sands Point, New York, she met Michelle Smithdas, a young woman who had lost her hearing at age sixteen due to a congenital defect, and her sight at age twenty-two in a snowmobiling accident.

At the time of her accident, Michelle was a senior at Gallaudet University in Washington, D.C., the only college for deaf students in the United States. Michelle had managed to finish her B.A. from Gallaudet and become an assistant instructor at the Helen Keller Center. But she wanted to get her master's degree and become a full instructor. After two frustrating attempts at taking the necessary courses, first at New York University, and then at Hofstra University, Michelle had just about given up.

Linda, on hearing Michelle's story, decided to take on the challenge as if it were her own. She researched schools and discovered that the one with the type of courses Michelle needed was Columbia Teachers College. Linda approached the head of the graduate program and was able to get Michelle accepted. Knowing that it would be tough under any circumstances, Linda set about the task of making sure Michelle would succeed. She purchased two sets of books— one for herself and the other to be torn into individual chapters to be translated into braille for Michelle's use.

Each day, Linda drove Michelle the twenty or so miles into Manhattan to attend classes, all the time communicating through "finger spelling," the process of forming symbols in another person's palm with your own fingers and knuckles.

While sitting through the lectures, the women would sometimes "chat" about what the other students were wearing, or make jokes. They were sometimes reprimanded for Michelle's raucous laughter. The two women became very close friends, and what really made the difference for Michelle was that Linda was always there for her.

Perhaps the most moving demonstration of Linda's devotion was her reaction to the news that she might have a cancerous tumor growing through her own optic nerve. Although she was frightened for herself, she was more concerned about the effect it would have on Michelle.

"Michelle is depending on me to help her get her master's degree," she explained. "I couldn't let her down."

Linda scheduled her surgery during the winter break to avoid disrupting Michelle's classes. Fortunately, the tumor was benign, and Linda's eyesight was unaffected. During her recovery, the two women missed only one class.

Michelle eventually graduated with a master's degree in education for the blind and visually impaired. For Linda, helping Michelle get her master's degree equaled the work of a five-year part-time job. But both agree that Michelle could not have done it without her.

For her efforts Linda wanted nothing other than the pleasure of seeing Michelle accomplish what she had set out to do.

"It was time-consuming," Linda admits, "but I loved it. Helping Michelle was the best thing I ever did. It was the highlight of my life."

Linda not only led Michelle to greater self-reliance by enabling her to do what she had always wanted to do; she also contributed to every student Michelle will eventually teach.

As this story demonstrates, the opportunities for service are as varied as the people who give of themselves. Volunteers in our national forests, national parks, and wildlife refuges maintain hiking trails, clear scrub, provide emergency rescue services, or simply act as guides. Guides in our museums help visitors appreciate fine art. Volunteers in libraries teach literacy. Many schools have programs that bring mentors together with struggling students. The list of opportunities available is only as limited as our imagination. And there are opportunities the entire family can share in as easily and effectively as an individual. Service is a wonderful way of involving children in the spirit of giving, from a very early age. Our two daughters, ages nine and twelve, help in a first-grade classroom every two weeks, and our son, age fifteen, sings and plays guitar in a band for high school worship at church. By encouraging our children to serve, we can set the right example and *do* what is right at the same time.

A hefty bank account or a particular genius is not a prerequisite to service. What is necessary is a desire to help and to serve.

For a number of years, our family had the tradition of joining my mother-in-law and my late father-in-law, Elsa and Ed Prince, working at a local senior citizen center that they had founded. Every year we helped prepare and serve Thanksgiving dinner to seniors in the community who had nowhere else to go, and then we cleaned up afterward. It was a family affair that spanned three generations as grandparents, parents, and grandchildren served the seniors and gave thanks for our many blessings as a family. We believe when we serve others, we are serving God, as did Jesus, who said that he came to serve and not to be served. The Christian call to action is actually a call to service.

People committed to service do not look for rewards, only the knowledge that their efforts are making a difference. Listening to the quiet thanks of seniors after our Thanksgiving dinner and seeing the look on their faces made our efforts there all worthwhile. Another positive outcome of service is making new friends and working closely together with others who share common goals, values, and interests. For example, I found leading a Boy Scout troop to be very rewarding, as it gave me the opportunity to work with a group of other leaders whose company I enjoyed and from whom I learned a great deal.

Perhaps the most important rewards of service are the intangible results of giving something back to our communities. This has been the philosophy of Bill Kellogg, the president of General Packaging Products of Chicago, and the great-grandson of the founder of Kellogg's cereals. Despite a schedule that would overwhelm most people, Kellogg teaches English one day a week at inner-city schools. He is reportedly such a popular teacher that there is a waiting list to get into his classes.

A man who shares Kellogg's commitment to his community is Arthur Kaplan, a judge on the Atlanta Municipal Court by day and a volunteer emergency medic at night. For thirty-eight years Kaplan has volunteered his services as an emergency medical technician, during which time he has treated nearly thirty thousand injuries and won seven Red Cross awards for saving people's lives. For people like Kellogg and Kaplan, service is a way to acknowledge the debt owed to our nation and to the generations that went before us, and to help prepare future generations to meet challenges.

There are times when our needs go beyond our abilities to help ourselves, and help from others becomes essential. Denny Whelan, one of our country's most respected private detectives, knows this well. Although he earned his reputation by tracking down murderers, it was a kidnapping case that put him in the national spotlight as a man who puts service before all else.

At the time of the kidnapping, Whelan was a volunteer youth counselor in Omaha, Nebraska, who had committed himself to helping kids in trouble. Troubled youths could relate to Whelan for the same reason that Whelan related to them: in his youth, "Kid Terror," as Whelan had been called, had been an alcoholic and a drug abuser. Had someone not reached out to help him, he surely would have been dead or in prison. Now, as a youth counselor, he was helping others. Young people cared for him because he cared for them. He would help anyone he could, no questions asked, and with no reward except the pleasure of returning some of the help that he had been given.

Among the many community-based outreach programs he helped to pioneer was a shelter for troubled teenagers, which served as a counseling center for alcohol and drug abusers, as well as a medical and legal referral service. But Whelan's sideline was reuniting runaway children with their parents, a service he undertook on a volunteer basis. It was for this reason that the family of thirteen-year-old Todd Bequette came to see Whelan.

The Bequettes didn't believe that Todd had run away. They were convinced that he had been kidnapped, but neither the police nor the FBI was willing to look into the case.

"This is not normally what I do," Whelan told the parents. "But if your boy needs help, I'll see that he gets it."

Whelan's only lead was a collect telephone call that Todd made to his stepbrother, in which he said he had run away and requested that the family not send the police looking for him. Whelan's experience had taught him that such a call was usually not what it appeared to be. At least not from a thirteen-year-old child who had disappeared at a bus stop.

Whelan traced the call to a motel room in northern Nebraska. His investigation revealed that the room had been

rented by a man named Terry Holman, whom police identified as a convicted sex offender and a suspect in the murders
of at least five children and young adults. Holman had been
seen there in the company of a teenage boy who fit Todd's
description.

Using telephone and welfare records, Whelan tracked
Holman through Iowa and Colorado and four other states.
But each time he got close, Holman, using forged identification, vanished to another city. Whelan counted twenty-two
different names that Holman used in a period of a year and
a half.

A young girl in Trinidad, Colorado, finally recognized
Todd's picture from a flyer that Whelan had distributed.
Holman managed to elude Whelan once again, but then a
paper trail led to a small cabin in Clarkson, Washington.

"I cried when I opened the door to that cabin and found
that boy alive," Whelan said. "It was the proudest moment in
my life because I knew that I had made a difference. I knew
that my life had counted for something."

Holman was arrested and Todd, now sixteen years old,
was reunited with his parents.

Service may be performed in a simple thought or gesture,
or in a dramatic manner, as demonstrated by Denny Whelan.
The important thing to remember is what the English poet
Robert Browning noted, "All service ranks the same with
God."

When we serve others, we contribute to freedom in many
different ways, and in doing so, we help make the world a
better place.

## 20

# Charity

As noted in the previous chapter, time, talent, and energy are gifts we give in service. These same gifts, transformed by our work into financial resources, are given in charity.

Although the personal commitment to serving others is very important, sometimes we aren't the best person to take on a particular job. Not all of us have the expertise, training, or resources necessary to meet every need. I, for example, am not qualified to work with a homeless alcoholic, even though I may have the compassion or desire to do so. I don't have the experience or training to be of real service. However, I, along with many others, have been blessed with the financial resources to support those who do.

Those who do have the expertise need our support to perform their work, to pay for the costs of their programs, and to provide for their families.

Charity is voluntary sacrifice on the part of private citizens. And, like service, private charity has had a long and meaningful tradition in our country. Americans have more nonprofit organizations than any other country, and they give more per person than any other country. In 1995, Americans gave more than $126 billion to charities—a record high. And the baby-boomer generation, often considered too self-indulgent to care much for their fellow citizens, gave the greatest portion of those dollars.

This wellspring of giving in our country is firmly rooted in compassion and the commitment to preserving freedom. Contrary to popular belief, a recent study shows that Americans do not give less when the tax incentives go down, but, in fact, have been known to give more.

Many Americans believe, as I do, that it is not only their right, but their duty to see to the welfare of others. By welfare I don't mean government subsidies to the poor. I believe the highest form of charity is helping people help themselves. Despite growing reliance on the government by many of our citizens, the vast majority of us still believe it is up to individuals and private groups to reach out and provide assistance from within our own communities. This requires more than lip service. It means "putting our money where our mouth is."

Many great Americans have done just that. Andrew Carnegie, a Scottish immigrant and self-made millionaire, established more than 2,500 libraries in small towns and cities across America through his philanthropy. He did this because he believed everyone in America should have the opportunity to get an education.

Another famous American who has contributed greatly to his country reflects this tradition of charity at its finest. However, I'm not going to tell you his name at this point because I want you to look at his story from a fresh vantage point.

This man was born in the middle of the last century, the son of a poor New York peddler. From his father he learned how to earn and save money. From his mother he learned to put God first in his life, to be honest and charitable.

He said of himself: "From the beginning I was trained to work, to save, and to give."

From the first day at his first job as a bookkeeper, earning fifty cents a day, he had a commitment to honest business practices. And from his first paycheck he gave ten percent to his church, a foreign mission, and the poor. He did the same at his second job, and his third.

As a teenager, he joined a fellow church member in the growing industry of oil refining. He concentrated on producing a quality product by putting his profits back into the business and was able to produce kerosene so cheaply that it became the most efficient lighting source for American homes, streets, and factories. For the first time in history, working-class people could afford to light their homes at night. By the turn of the century, working and reading after dark became activities almost all Americans could enjoy.

Continuing his philosophy of efficiency and keeping down costs, the young industrialist purchased the inefficient operations of his competitors and turned them around, helping the price of kerosene to drop from twenty-six cents to eight cents a gallon. He ended by owning one of the largest oil companies in the world.

Yet the more money he made, the more he gave away. By the time he died, he'd given away $550 million, more than any other American before him had even possessed, let alone given to charity. Beyond the sharing of his wealth, his production of affordable fuels for lighting homes and powering cars enhanced every American's quality of life. That man, by the way, was John D. Rockefeller.

Because of people like him and others, much has been done to build our nation through charitable donations. My own wonderful parents have set a great example for our family as well as for the West Michigan community. Through their generous support of so many civic, artistic, and social-welfare efforts, they have led the way for many. A children's hospital, a performing arts center, an international business school, and a graduate school all bear their names in thanks and recognition for their generous contributions.

My late father- (as well as mother-in-law) believed so strongly in the concept of giving that he bought out a partner in the early days of his business rather than change the company policy that a portion of all profits were to be given to charitable endeavors. My parents and parents-in-law have been firm believers in making personal sacrifices by giving back to their communities.

The question we need to ask ourselves is, How much is enough? My own Judeo-Christian tradition encourages a ten percent tithe of one's income. This serves as a good guideline and a good starting point. But we should all strive to do more. Betsy and I have consistently put more than ten percent of our income into a foundation that is earmarked for charitable giving. We have many causes we like to support, from think tanks to Christian evangelism to student scholarships. Four times a year we sit down to review requests and to consider proposals for new programs we may want to support.

We view giving as a joy and a requirement of service and sacrifice. Just as we must forgive because we have been forgiven, we must also give because God has given so abundantly to us.

Indeed, the true value of a gift to the giver is the extent to which the gift requires sacrifice. Mother Teresa states it this way: "When your gift becomes a sacrifice, it will have value toward God." The smallest of gifts can be the most significant when that is all the giver has to give. The New Testament story of the widow's mite illustrates this. In the story, a poor widow was embarrassed by the small amount of money she was able to give to her church, in contrast to a wealthy businessman who had given a large amount of money. Yet the Lord found more favor in her gift because she had given all she had.

Giving is not about the size of the gift, but the size of the heart of the giver. Hyrum Smith, chairman of the board of the Franklin Quest Company, whose daily and weekly planners are sold by Amway and used by many of our employees and distributors, captures the spirit of this in a story that he relates about his childhood.

Hyrum grew up on one of the Hawaiian Islands in a family of seven children that was rich in spirit but poor in material resources. When Hyrum was eight years old, his family's financial condition became so critical that his parents were concerned they wouldn't be able to celebrate Christmas in the same way they had done in previous years. However, all seven of the children were assured they would each receive one gift, and they were asked to choose what their gift would be.

Hyrum gave great thought to what he would ask for, then

told his mother and father that what he really wanted most of all was a bushel of apples.

His parents were surprised by the request. As much as Hyrum loved apples, he couldn't possibly eat an entire bushel. Moreover, apples didn't grow in Hawaii. They had to be shipped from the mainland, and were both difficult to get and rather expensive. Despite his parents' difficulty in obtaining his gift, Hyrum found a bushel of apples—with each apple wrapped in individual yellow tissue—waiting under the tree on Christmas day.

Hyrum was ecstatic. As soon as the rest of his family had opened presents, he took his bushel of apples and went off to visit his friends and neighbors. When he returned home, the basket was empty. He had shared his gift, and had known as much joy in giving as he had in receiving. Hyrum had never felt better. Others had enjoyed the apples as much as he had.

As we get older and are able to give more, the issue broadens beyond the act of giving to include the responsibility of knowing that what is being given will actually lead to long-term benefits for others. It's easy to see the benefits of buying medical supplies, basketballs, and schoolbooks. These are important and worthwhile causes. But a great many of us question the wisdom of continually providing goods and services that don't help enable others to take charge of their lives, potentially leaving them in a state of dependence.

A key ingredient I like about charitable giving is that it is not forced redistribution. It is completely voluntary and helps both the giver and the receiver—it comes out of the heart rather than from an impersonal government system.

Obviously there will always be those who are not and never will be able to become capable and self-reliant: the very ill, the mentally handicapped, and the very old. Then there are children, who cannot care for themselves, but if taught properly, will be able to take care of themselves one day. One of the best-known medieval rabbis, Maimonides, listed helping people to take care of themselves as the *highest* level of charity. I agree. True charity, for those who are capable, is a hand up rather than a handout. And while some may need to be dependent for a short while, it should not become a permanent condition.

An excellent example of a program that promotes self-reliance can be found in Grand Rapids, Michigan. The Inner City Christian Federation works with homeless and low-income families to help them become homeowners. Through careful management of renovation and new construction projects, the federation is able to sell housing at affordable prices to qualified buyers, using low-rate mortgages as financing. A qualified buyer is someone who has successfully completed an instructional program that teaches people about the responsibilities of home ownership, such as making mortgage payments, paying taxes, and handling maintenance, repairs, and budgeting. Instead of being "given" a home, the people work to make themselves qualified home buyers and eventually homeowners who are equipped with the skills and confidence to remain that way all of their lives.

The expectation of continuous charity sometimes leads people to behave in ways that simply sustain their dependence. When we give the fish, instead of the fishing rod, it sends the hidden message that we do not believe they can fish for themselves. This is why it is important to know exactly where our charitable gifts go and how they are being spent. Confirming that our money is being well spent may require a trip to the soup kitchen to learn more about the program we are supporting or it might require looking at the financial statements to see how much of our money is going to services versus administration. To be effective stewards of our charity, the people and organizations we support must be financially and operationally accountable.

Each of us needs to become personally involved in meeting the needs of our communities. Although it's easy to find stories of the wealthy and financially successful giving to charity, giving is something everyone can do. I was always taught that I should handle whatever money I had with an open hand. Whatever we have is not really ours; it is only given to us in trust, by God, and must be cared for and shared in a responsible fashion.

One man who has learned this kind of responsible generosity is Ed Huber, a restaurateur who became owner of Delmonico's, the famous New York steak house whose illustrious list of diners has included Charles Dickens, Mark Twain, Lillian Russell, Diamond Jim Brady, and every president from James Monroe to Franklin D. Roosevelt.

Huber had owned several successful New York restaurants before a friend told him that the old Delmonico's property in lower Manhattan's Wall Street area was available. The boarded-up property on Beaver Street had been turned into an apartment building and then had been sitting vacant for five years. As soon as Huber saw the building, he knew he wanted it; he wanted to restore Delmonico's to its former glory. He leased the building, and at great personal expense restored its Victorian dining room with its leaded windows, crystal chandeliers, and dark wood paneling. He then gutted the basement and put in a second dining room with a gracefully curved staircase. The new Delmonico's was an instant hit, and Huber was ecstatic—that is, until he discovered that the John Heuss House, a homeless shelter, was scheduled to be opened three doors down.

Huber entertained visions of the many ways the shelter would destroy the seven years of energy, work, and capital he had invested in Delmonico's. He pictured winos and bag ladies lined up outside his restaurant, panhandling his customers. "It's not that I didn't feel for the homeless," Huber said. "I just didn't want them in my backyard."

Huber fought the installation of the homeless shelter in every way that he could. Most significantly, he formed a coalition of business owners and concerned residents that held press conferences, demonstrated, and finally went so far as pursuing legal action in an effort to block the shelter.

The rector of Wall Street's Trinity Church, which was going to operate the shelter, decided to bring both sides together, hoping they might find some common ground. For Huber, it was a humbling experience. He saw, for the first time, exactly what it was that Trinity Church was trying to do: to honor the humanity of the poor. Panhandling was not on the Trinity Church agenda. Huber also met Winfield Peacock, the dynamic Presbyterian minister who was going to manage the shelter. By the end of the meeting, Huber had swallowed his pride and was asking what he could do to help.

Help he did. Not only did he join other residents and business leaders in serving on an advisory board to the shelter, but he also gave his help and support in other ways. A few days after the shelter's opening he began making early-morning deliveries of day-old food, which would have gone to waste. Later, when the shelter's meat slicer broke down, he offered them the use of the one at Delmonico's.

The giving became contagious. The dishwasher broke and Huber sent the Delmonico's mechanic to fix it. When Huber told the contractor to put the repairs on his bill, the contractor said that he would donate his services. Other business owners and many of Delmonico's customers got into the act, channeling money, equipment, and time to the shelter.

As this story demonstrates, charity comes in a surprising variety of forms. Penny Thomas, of Accokeek, Maryland, exercised a most unique form of charity. Penny had been waiting desperately for the liver transplant that would save the life of her six-year-old daughter, Candi. But when the liver was finally available, Penny and her husband allowed it to be given to a child whose condition was even worse than their own daughter's, a child who would surely die unless she received it. They performed this generous act without any assurance that another liver would become available, or that their own child would live long enough for a transplant. Thankfully in the end, both children lived.

A final story that illustrates the great wellspring of giving that can come from everyone—no matter what their income— is that of Dale and Kelly Clem and their church in Piedmont, Alabama.

Kelly met her husband-to-be at Duke Divinity School. Both had their sights set on becoming ministers, and soon, both had their sights set on one another as well. They married and moved to Alabama, where they became associate ministers at a church in Huntsville.

The year after their first child, Hannah, was born, the

Clems moved to Piedmont, where Kelly became the pastor of the Goshen United Methodist Church. There Sarah, their second child, was born.

Having a woman head the 135-member congregation was something new to the people in Piedmont, but once the parishioners figured out what to call Kelly (Pastor), everything went along fine. Kelly's congregation was thriving and their children were growing up in a loving and supportive community as their lives settled into good and dependable rhythms.

Then came the Palm Sunday when everything changed.

Dale, who was campus minister at local Jacksonville University, had taken a group of college students on a hiking excursion in Oklahoma. Four-year-old Hannah, who loved helping her mom, insisted on going to the church with her to help prepare for the services.

The church was crowded, and by late in the morning worship, close to 11:30, the Palm Sunday pageant was well under way and hymns filled the air.

Hannah was sitting on the opposite side of the church from her mother, and there were other children sitting in the pew with her. Nearby sat a mother and her eight-year-old son. Toward the back of the church was Sarah, with the baby-sitter.

Suddenly, the lights went out. The hymns trailed off as the assembled worshipers craned their necks, wondering what was going on. Then other, more sinister sounds began filling the church. First came the staccato drumming of heavy rain on the roof, then heavy hail. Then came the sound of breaking glass as a window gave way.

A lone voice called out, "Everybody down! Tornado!" Moments later, a churning swirl of devastation struck full force, tearing the building to pieces. Walls collapsed, bricks and timbers became deadly projectiles, and pews were thrown about like dollhouse furniture.

When Kelly was finally able to stand, she had blood running down her face and a dislocated shoulder. Kelly was desperate to find her daughters.

She stumbled to where she thought Hannah might be, but nothing was in the same place. It looked as though a bomb had been detonated, shredding everything and everyone.

Then, she spotted Hannah. What drew Kelly's attention was Hannah's pink dress and tights. But the little girl was now under a heavy pew. Sprawled across the top of the pew was the body of another child.

Kelly pawed at the rubble, but Hannah's lifeless body was cold, limp, and had already taken on the gray tint of death.

"I remember looking up and somebody was showing me Sarah," Kelly recalls. "She was okay."

As Kelly sat stunned, through her haze she could see the eight-year-old boy sitting in the rubble. His mother, now dead, lay next to him. Through desperate tears, he wailed, "You can't die, Mom. I'm only eight years old." Even though Kelly could see it was hopeless, for the sake of the boy she crawled over and administered CPR to the lifeless body of his mother.

More than seven hundred miles away, in Lawton, Oklahoma, word of the disaster got to Dale Clem. When he was finally able to reach his wife by telephone, he received the worst news of his life: his eldest daughter, Hannah, was gone. He caught the first flight out.

Dale's return plunged him into the maelstrom of activity that had been left in the wake of the tornado. In the church and surrounding community, twenty people had died as a result of the tornado, wreaking havoc in the lives of everyone in the region. The entire congregation was racked with grief, and the Clems provided counseling, comfort, and caring words. And in the midst of all this, they had their own grieving to do and their daughter's funeral to arrange.

"We had supernatural strength," Kelly recounts. "I kept telling people, 'Your prayers are getting us through.' "

The Lord responded to the prayers in a way unimagined by those praying. In addition to the emotional support he provided to the grieving families, out of the heap of the debris that was once their church, an American phenomenon took place. No sooner had news of the tragedy spread than a line of cars started filling the church parking lot. Still others were on the interstate, heading toward the church. People came from all over the state to offer their condolences. They also offered financial support. Many made withdrawals from savings accounts and retirement plans. They brought their milk money, paper route earnings, and piggy banks. There were big gifts and little gifts.

Nothing could bring back the lives of those who had been lost, but the gifts amounted to enough that the people of Piedmont were able to honor the memory of their loved ones by building a new church.

Through personal service and charity, we are able to do so much good for others in need, whether helping to change a chronic situation or, as in this case, helping those in a crisis. Charity can multiply and transform our time, energy, and talent in meaningful ways, allowing us to contribute to freedom in ways which would normally be beyond our own capability.

## ❧ 21 ❧

# Leadership

Like charity, leadership is also a form of service. Leaders can serve others by motivating and helping them to develop integrity and self-reliance and by helping them to create, articulate, recognize, and uphold their own goals and the goals of those they influence.

Leaders can be born, and they can be developed. The ability to lead can be developed if the desire to serve is there, but the commitment to personal integrity must be unshakable. Those who take on leadership roles simply for the sake of control, wealth, or fame are often dangerous in those positions. And while skill in diplomacy can be a great leadership asset, the most important requirements, other than the desire to serve, are the ability to carry a vision, to be trustworthy, and to have courage.

In the current environment, there seems to be a trend

away from leadership and toward management. This even includes our national elected leadership. Many Americans today seem to be looking for a manager rather than a true leader, even in the White House. Our leaders should not only be competent administrators, but more importantly, they should provide vision and proactive direction.

Inspirational leaders bring out the best in us. They challenge us to do more than we thought possible, and they inspire us with vision. But we cannot forget that if leaders are headed in the wrong direction, they can also lead an entire nation to ruin. Therefore, we must hold them accountable.

Leaders play a significant stewardship role since they must make decisions on behalf of other citizens. It naturally follows, then, that they must also be held accountable. This entails the accountability that comes with upholding the freedom and rights of others as well as personal accountability for the use of freedom and the example they set.

Our country needs inspirational leaders who can courageously articulate a vision, be trustworthy, and steer us in a direction that is consistent with our values, goals, and aspirations.

A leader must be consistent in both personal and public standards. Trustworthy leaders are people whose private lives are not in direct conflict with their public lives. While few people are above reproach in all aspects of their lives, we should be very concerned about leaders whose private lives differ substantially from their public persona.

We must be willing to accept the imperfections of our leaders, but it is essential that the lives they live are consistent with who they say they are. For example, a candidate for public office who talks about upholding families shouldn't be in the midst of a third divorce. Inconsistency between what candidates say and what they do indicates that they are untrustworthy—either because of a lack of integrity or the lack of a moral compass and the strength to do what is right.

When there is significant inconsistency between word and action, it is difficult to imagine such a person doing what is right. And while we must be careful not to set unrealistic standards for our leaders, we should ask whether they repeatedly make the same mistakes, or learn from their mistakes and change their behavior. If they demonstrate that they learn from their mistakes, they will become better leaders.

The only people who don't make mistakes in life are those who don't take risks and avoid responsibility for decisions. They are not leaders!

As in all challenging positions, good leadership develops out of hard work and experience. For this reason, it concerns me that many of our elected officials have never worked outside of politics. So many don't know what it is like to spend and risk their own resources when making decisions, nor have they gained the experience and understanding that comes with working in the private sector.

America has produced many great leaders from all walks of life and positions of responsibility. Often we find people in subordinate roles who take initiative and, through the results of their hard work, earn positions of leadership. A community leader who earned that right is Janice Robertson, a housewife in the Flatlands section of Brooklyn, New York.

"I am an American," Janice L. Robertson is proud to say. "And what I want is nothing different from what any other American wants: a safe place to live, good schools for my children, a good life for my family. If it takes a fight, then so be it."

Janice Robertson is an African American woman who, along with her husband, Leonard, moved their family into a neighborhood that, as it turned out, was almost all white.

The Robertsons left their old neighborhood of Ebbets Field because it was overrun with drugs and gangs. Janice and Leonard and their three boys—Leonard, Dario, and Rashaan, affectionately known as Ruti—decided on a nice house with a front porch and a big backyard on sunny, tree-lined East Forty-ninth Street, in the Flatlands. Although their old neighborhood was only fifteen minutes away, their new one—with its pretty parks and good schools—seemed to be a world apart. With some help from Janice's dad, they were able to buy the house. They thought they were living the American dream.

But the dream didn't last long. A few days after they moved in, Janice found white paint splattered across the front of their home. Although it had not occurred to her before, the reality of what had happened suddenly sank in. They were the only African American family on the block and one of only a few black families in the entire neighborhood.

The overt harassment had begun. Local toughs spat on the boys as they walked along the streets. Dario was warned by some of the locals not to play baseball in the public park. The boys were constantly tormented and called names. Then their home was vandalized a second time. Their new neighborhood was turning out to be just as dangerous as their old one. They were shocked that people they had assumed to be just hardworking citizens like themselves would behave like this.

They also thought that such things only happened in the old days of racism.

After several months, a white woman knocked on the Robertsons' door and told Janice that she had overheard some neighbors talking about burning them out. The woman was having trouble with her conscience and felt that she could not remain silent. She revealed to Janice the names of the people involved.

Armed with this information, Janice did a remarkable thing. She went to those people's homes, one by one, and confronted them. Some would not answer the door. Others denied any involvement. Many of them looked embarrassed and angry at getting caught. Apparently, the fact that Janice arrived on their front steps and looked them in the eye put a stop to the plot in the planning stages.

The next year, at age forty, Janice had her fourth child, another boy, whom she named Curtis. She decided to give up the studies she had undertaken and stay at home. If her children got hurt, she wanted to be there for them.

A few years later, Ruti, then in eighth grade, was attacked. He had been standing at a bus stop with several other children. Although there had been a group of white kids across the street, he had barely noticed them. Just as the bus arrived, the kids from across the street swarmed around Ruti and the others, wielding sticks with nails, metal pipes, and rocks. Along with the children who were waiting with him, Ruti jumped aboard the bus, desperately seeking shelter. He narrowly missed having his skull crushed by a length of lead pipe. As the attackers broke out the windows and shouted epithets, the bus driver called the police on the bus phone.

But by the time the police arrived, the thugs had disappeared into waiting getaway cars.

Janice remembers the time of the incident clearly. After seeing the fear in Ruti's face and feeling the terror at having nearly lost her son, she called authorities, but got little action. The city's Bias Investigation Unit declared the incident "menacing," but had no suspects, so they closed the case without further action.

Janice knew full well that the incident was an organized attempt to drive them and other African Americans from the neighborhood. Again, Janice decided to take the problem door to door.

Every morning after she sent her husband and the older boys on their way, Janice took her baby and went from house to house, block by block. Sometimes she was ignored and addressed rudely. But she kept on talking to her neighbors about bringing all the people of the community together. Finally, it began to sink in.

"I told them what had happened to my son, Ruti. Most of them were shocked and concerned," she recounts. "They had nothing to do with it, but they'd never opened their mouths to speak out either. I told them that when you have violent people in a community, the ones who stand quiet aid and abet them."

The more Janice talked with her neighbors, the more they listened. And she learned a lot from them too. For instance, the neighborhood had other problems that concerned everyone, such as poor sanitation services, increasing criminal activity, and other undesirable developments.

Janice decided that what the neighborhood needed was a block association, and she was just the person to form it. She printed and handed out flyers, asking people to meet at a local synagogue. This meeting, the very first of the East Forty-ninth Street Block Association of Flatlands Inc., was attended by three hundred people. Since then, Janice has served several terms as the association's president.

The association's accomplishments are many and significant to those in the ten-block area served by its existence. Some shining examples include getting the construction of an hourly-rate motel stopped and getting the neighborhood's city services upgraded. Now there is a sense of involvement and caring among the neighbors. When there are suspicious activities, someone is sure to investigate, just to make certain that their neighbors are all right.

"There are always going to be things that can erode a community," Janice explains. "The only way to solve our problems is as a group."

The Robertsons' boys are older now, with Leonard and Dario both out of college and working in the King's County district attorney's office. Ruti has graduated from college and is working for the largest environmental law firm in New York State, located in Albany. Curtis is in junior high school. And when Janice walks down the streets of her neighborhood these days, she's waved to and greeted with smiles.

Janice says that all of this began "once we began to focus on the things we had in common, rather than the things that made us different."

Janice understood the role common goals play in keeping a community together, and she courageously took the lead in helping her neighborhood find them and work toward them.

Since leaders must often make decisions that impact

others, one of their responsibilities is unique: open communication with their constituents and all those who are affected by their decisions. I call this "transparency." As discussed in the chapter on honesty, when someone has incomplete or inaccurate information, it is difficult for them to make good decisions. This is true for both leaders and their constituents.

When significant decisions are pending, it's important that constituents be aware of them and the process that goes into making them. But the need for transparency goes both ways. It means that constituents must be able to receive information and to give relevant feedback and input on the pending decision.

Leaders can sometimes consciously use transparency to teach by example. By being open about their own trials and tribulations and how they overcame them, they can make their experiences both instructive and inspiring to others. Benjamin Franklin knew this well. He took every opportunity to offer instruction and suggestions to others on how to better oneself. This mentoring is an important aspect of leadership.

A more recent example of a person who has served to teach through inspiration rather than by instruction is Betty Ford, a good friend and former resident of my hometown of Grand Rapids, as well as the adored First Lady and wife of former President Gerald Ford. When Betty was diagnosed with breast cancer and subsequently had a breast removed, she decided that breast cancer was a topic that had been "hush-hush" for far too long.

While still in the White House, Betty had gone to see her doctor for a routine checkup, only to discover she had a lump in her breast. Within a little over twenty-four hours she was in surgery. When she came out of the anesthetic she discovered that doctors had found cancer in three of her lymph nodes as well as in one of her breasts, and that breast had been removed.

Betty Ford could have maintained a great deal more secrecy than she did about her own tragedy, but she knew that her experience could be invaluable to thousands of other women. She also knew she was in a unique position to reach them. As she said, "If I hadn't been the wife of the president of the United States, the press would not have come racing after me." It took great courage on her part to share this personal and painful experience with the world.

Until that time, breast cancer was seldom discussed, and millions of women went year after year without proper breast examinations. Betty courageously broke the silence and gave interviews about her condition.

As a result, thousands of women began having breast examinations. Happy Rockefeller, wife of Vice President Nelson Rockefeller, was one of them. Three weeks after the president's wife had a mastectomy, so did Happy. Today, Shirley Temple Black, Nancy Reagan, Olivia Newton-John, my sister-in-law Joan, and thousands of other women have discovered the presence of the disease before it could take their lives.

Perhaps more than anything else, Betty Ford's leadership has been instrumental in bringing women's health-care issues to the forefront of public attention. It took even greater courage when she revealed that, after years of taking medications, she had developed an addiction to alcohol and prescription drugs.

Again, Betty led a national discussion on a subject that had long been kept under wraps: the recognition of addiction as a serious problem throughout our nation. Her message was that there is no shame in having a problem as long as you face it and get help. Her leadership and courage undoubtedly saved the lives of many individuals.

"I tried to be honest," Betty said of the interviews. "I tried not to dodge subjects. I felt the public had a right to know where I stood. Nobody had to feel the way I felt. I wasn't forcing my opinions on anybody, but if someone asked me a question, I gave that person a straight answer."

Thanks to her candor in discussing these subjects, going for help became acceptable and recognized as the route to take when facing addictions and substance abuse.

Betty Ford clearly understood the special role she could play in leading the nation toward better management of some of our health-care issues. In her case, rather than shun the transparency that came with her prominence, she used it as a teaching tool for the good of the nation.

Leadership is one of those roles people sometimes accept without understanding the responsibilities they carry. Today there are people in leadership positions who operate without integrity or accountability, and without understanding their roles as stewards. And frequently, they do not understand the necessity of transparency.

This is why it is so important for us to first know what values our leaders hold, to understand their vision, and to be comfortable with the actions they would take toward that vision. If we do not ascertain these things, we will elect or promote leaders who may not share our ideals.

For Christians, Jesus is the ultimate leader. His example gives me the strong moral compass that keeps me on track and enables me to withstand the pressures that criticism and temptation create. His model of "servant leadership" is the model I aspire to emulate.

I believe it is important to know to what extent a spiritual commitment is present in our leaders. It helps us to better understand the compass that directs them.

Whether leadership is demonstrated in our communities, our businesses, or within our homes, the same principles apply. True leaders leave a legacy: they pass the mantle of leadership to others who are inspired by their vision and convictions and will carry on.

Great leaders can do significant things individually and collectively. Through demonstrating integrity and utilizing their God-given abilities, leaders contribute toward securing greater freedoms in society. They also inspire us to be self-reliant, to accomplish our goals, and to live lives of integrity, thus realizing our full potential.

As President Harry S. Truman once said about leaders, they "make history and not the other way round. In periods where there is no leadership, society stands still. Progress occurs when courageous, skillful leaders seize the opportunity to change things for the better."

## 22

# Opportunity

Opportunity exists in America because we are a nation of free people. In this discussion about rediscovering America's values, I have shared the stories of people who have enjoyed opportunities afforded by our nation's freedom. In fact, most of the stories in this book are about opportunity. People like fifth-grade teacher Bessie Pender, skater Kristi Yamaguchi, and Tom Monaghan of Domino's all made commitments, worked hard, and persevered. But they also had opportunity.

It is precisely because of the opportunity this country offers that more people emigrate to the United States each year than to any other nation. And opportunity comes hand in hand with freedom. The more freedom we have, the more opportunity we have. Unlike in many other countries, the opportunity that exists in America permits a citizen to go from a level of extreme poverty to great wealth within his or her lifetime. However, it is also possible to go from great wealth right down to the poverty level just as quickly! For the purposes of this book, I will speak of opportunity from the perspective of moving upward, of getting ahead in life and reaching greater levels of opportunity.

Perhaps what America is best known for is the idea of equal opportunity. However, there has recently been confusion in the application of the concept of equal opportunity. Some interpret this to mean that everyone is entitled to the same things, whether they work for them or not. This has resulted in many ill-conceived programs that, under the banner of equality, do more to limit freedom than to enhance it.

While God created everyone in his image and likeness, not everyone is born with the same talents and abilities. Some people are blessed with beautiful voices, and others with a wonderful athletic ability or an ability to work well with people. But even if we were all born with the same talents, differences between us would quickly emerge by virtue of the freedom each of us has to choose how we use our talents. Even with identical abilities, a student unwilling to study will not receive the same grades as the diligent student. And an employee who is continually late for work and acts irresponsibly should not receive the same pay and promotions as his or her more reliable counterpart. Entitlement was not what our founding fathers had in mind. They were committed to protecting everyone's rights and opportunities, not to assuring everyone's "equal" success.

Although some people argue that opportunity in this country is becoming increasingly limited, some statistics don't support those claims. More than half of all CEOs of

*Fortune* 500 companies come from poor or lower-middle-class backgrounds. And eighty percent of our nation's millionaires have not inherited their wealth but earned their millions themselves, taking advantage of their freedom of opportunity.

Everyone can make a difference when it comes to opportunity. We should be constantly thinking in terms of expanding and upgrading and making more opportunities available for everybody—high school graduates, young adults coming out of college, immigrants, children at risk, and retired citizens. For something to truly be an opportunity, it must be available and within reach.

David and Falaka Fattah of Philadelphia have discovered the key to providing opportunity for members of inner-city gangs—individuals many would say have no opportunity. They are fierce believers in giving inner-city youth every opportunity possible: first, to escape the pitfalls of their environments, and then to develop the skills necessary to get ahead in life. The Fattahs have done this without turning to the government for help. For four years they cared for two hundred boys without any outside funding. (They now accept funds to cover the cost of food and clothing.)

David and Falaka didn't set out to initiate a novel solution to a serious neighborhood problem. They were just trying to keep their family intact when a nightmare descended upon them. What had cast the pall was a scourge that most urban parents pray will never lay claim to their children: street gangs. Tragically, in inner-city households like the Fattahs', it has become increasingly the rule rather than the exception.

When the Fattahs' teenage son, Robin, announced that he had joined the Clymer Street Gang, they were deeply troubled. But when they then discovered that he was considered the "heart" of the gang and a prime target for assassination, they became terrified. They knew that the gang struggle over territory was a never-ending cycle of murder and retribution. For them, it was not a question of whether their son would be killed or not, but only a question of when.

Falaka was determined not to let this happen. But she didn't know how to prevent what seemed to be the inevitable. At the time she was working for an African American journal called *Umoja* (Swahili for "unity of family") and had become increasingly educated on the many challenges of contemporary African American urban life. But the periodical had never tackled the topic of street gangs, and nothing in her background had prepared her to understand the dynamics of gang life.

Just the opposite was true of David. In his youth he had run with gangs, and he knew of their appeal to disenfranchised youth. But then the preferred means of settling disputes was one-on-one fistfights. The occasional stabbing was considered a shocking event.

The street scene had changed dramatically in the intervening years. Kids were now wielding semiautomatic weapons and were randomly spraying houses and groups of kids on the sidewalks with their deadly fusillades. What had once been macho posturing, costing an occasional broken nose or lost tooth, had become a dangerous battle for turf—a real matter of life and death.

One troubling aspect of the problem was that the Fattahs were unable to explain why, out of six sons, only this one would turn away from his loving family and toward the desperate peril of street-gang life.

Falaka and David had some tough choices to make. These were choices that, if wrongly made, could result in the loss of their son. Falaka searched for information. She wondered who was supposed to be doing something about the gang problem. Law enforcement didn't seem to be providing a solution, nor were churches or the many social service agencies.

"I found well-meaning people in the social services who weren't doing much," she recalled recently. "I found greedy people who were profiteering. I found politicians who were getting elected over the issue. But I didn't find anything going on that made me feel that my son would be safe."

To Falaka, those with the most vested interest in these problems were the people like herself who had sons or daughters who were members of a gang or lived in gang territory. But despite her research, she still could not comprehend why any kid would be attracted to gang life, to say nothing of being willing to die for the right to call a few square blocks of inner-city concrete their own. David tried to put it in perspective for her.

"Think of a gang as a family," he told her. He then pointed out that a lot of the kids joined because they didn't have a functioning family of their own.

"Well, if family is the problem," Falaka replied, "then family is the solution." She had a point, as she often did. David had long depended on his wife's levelheaded approach. But he was not prepared for what she would say next.

"Let the gang move in with us!" Falaka declared. "We'll give these guys an opportunity to see how a real family lives. It may save some lives. Most important, it'll save our son."

"You don't know what you're saying!" David warned her.

"It could be dangerous—for all of us." He went on to explain his real and quite justifiable concerns. Making one's home a gang headquarters was at best naive, and at worst potentially disastrous. They had five other sons to think of. Besides, there was not enough room for everyone to sleep in the house.

But Falaka was using her heart, and her deeply held faith in God. As a result of her unwavering conviction that it would work, that it must work, and her gentle but insistent persuasion, Falaka got her way.

In a matter of weeks, Crow, Peewee, Bird, and another dozen members of the Clymer Street Gang were calling the Fattahs' four-room house on Frazier Street their home.

At first, chaos ruled. The gang members slept late in the mornings and refused to help with housework. They failed to show up at mandatory "family" meetings. When the Fattahs pushed them to get some sort of part-time work, they complained that they couldn't find any.

Falaka and David were committed to the idea that, with a gentle but firm push in the right direction, the young men would come around. In the pursuit of that conviction, they had to take some risks.

In a family meeting, one of the gang members, Bird, announced that he and the others had composed the house rules by which they all would live. Falaka and David waited nervously. They had made the promise to abide by whatever rules the group came up with.

"No drinking, and no drugs," he began. "No girls in the rooms. No fighting." And here he paused, as the Fattahs held their collective breath. "And no more gang warring . . . ever."

Today, the Fattahs' "House of Umoja"—or Boystown—has successfully turned around three thousand former gang members. They lay claim to having given these boys sufficient opportunity to have transformed themselves into merchants, laborers, ministers, policemen, teachers, city officials, and a U.S. congressman.

The "house" now spreads over twenty-four buildings, with a paid staff that ranges from five on a more or less permanent basis, to dozens when necessary. Some are volunteers. And former "graduates" return regularly to counsel the youths who are following in their footsteps.

It should come as no surprise that the annual rate of gang-war deaths in Philadelphia dropped to negligible levels compared to the high of forty-three that David and Falaka faced when they began. And their son, Robin, is alive and well.

As David and Falaka can attest, the real value of their effort was in giving the gang members the opportunity to help themselves. While the Fattahs provided these kids with a "home," a base from which to grow, more importantly, they fostered the opportunity to grow toward integrity and self-reliance and to develop their abilities—the essential outgrowth of real freedom.

While some people need job opportunities, others need opportunities to develop greater self-reliance or greater skills in their areas of interest. The differences in talents and needs between us are vast. Some people simply need a business loan as an opportunity to change their destiny.

An American who has devoted his life to providing loans such as these is John Hatch, who has found an original and highly effective method for supporting freedom and opportunity abroad through the banking industry.

It's ironic that Hatch chose the banking business, for it has long been a popular and amusing notion that bankers will only lend money to those who don't need it. There's a kernel of truth here, especially when the people we're talking about are destitute Third World citizens who by traditional standards certainly would appear to be poor credit risks.

Not so, says Hatch, who put together the Foundation for International Community Assistance (FINCA). After more than twenty-eight years of experience in Third World development (twenty years of which were in the Peace Corps and at the Agency for International Development), this economist and Fulbright scholar started his own international aid program intended to meet the funding needs of the poor and to promote grassroots development by way of what are called "micro loans," small loans made directly to the local people for the purpose of getting local enterprises under way.

The concept of supporting freedom and opportunity abroad is not a new idea to the Hatch family. John's great-uncle on his mother's side was Minor Keith, a remarkable self-made man from Brooklyn who, in the late nineteenth century, built most of the railways in Central America, introduced the banana to the Americas, and was cofounder of the United Fruit Company. His father, Winslow Hatch, was a botany professor, college dean, and educator who himself claimed two illustrious ancestors: Peregrine White, the first baby born on the *Mayflower,* and Governor Winslow of the Plymouth Colony.

It is not surprising that Hatch, having come from such an illustrious family, should distinguish himself as an entrepreneur and unofficial ambassador to the Third World. And it was while working in this capacity, during his two decades of consulting with U.S. aid contractors, that Hatch witnessed what he described as a horrendous waste of foreign-aid dollars on rural development programs that failed to respect the individuality, self-determination, and expertise of the people they were supposed to help. He knew there was a better and cheaper way to help the world's poor help themselves, which is why he came up with the idea known as "village banking," which then became FINCA. Hatch used his own savings to get FINCA started, then worked for over four years to set up revolving loan programs in more than five hundred villages in Asia, Latin America, and Africa. Since then, the program has grown to serve twelve different countries.

The purpose of FINCA, as Hatch explains it, is to enhance the economic self-sufficiency of impoverished families who have been living on less than a few hundred dollars per year. FINCA helps people organize themselves into village banks, which finance the selling of fruits and vegetables, crafts, ceramics, and other market goods. FINCA village banks offer poor entrepreneurs three key services: access to self-employment loans of fifty to three hundred dollars, with no collateral required and a reasonable rate of interest; savings incentives and a plan to create three hundred dollars of their own working capital within three years; and group support for personal empowerment, which FINCA defines as a shift in attitude from "I can't" to "I can." The overall idea is to provide a loan, and not a gift, recognizing that loans foster discipline, responsibility, and initiative, while handouts or welfare destroy dignity and lead to dependency. Members of the village bank elect their own management committee, draft their own bylaws, keep their own books, manage all funds, supervise loan use, and are collectively responsible for repayment of capital.

It is interesting to note that the vast majority of village banks are owned and controlled by women. Hatch himself explains why.

"Nearly half of all impoverished families in the Third World depend on income generated by women. When given the opportunity, women are responsible borrowers, diligent savers, and competent managers who use their income to benefit their children."

Hatch's observations are backed up by the statistics. An incredible ninety-five percent pay back what they borrow. Of the twelve countries in which the program operates, seven report one hundred percent repayment.

What some considered a questionable idea now funds village banks through funding from foundations, banks, government sources, service clubs, churches, and private individuals. Country programs are designed to become fully self-financing from interest income within three years.

Although it appears on the surface to be an economic matter, a compelling reality underlying the reason for the program is the fact that, according to UNICEF's State of the World's Children Report, each day forty thousand children under five years of age die from chronic malnutrition or hunger-related disease. They are the victims of severe poverty, most often caused by an economic system that ignores free-market principles. A mother's ability to raise an additional five dollars a week makes a significant difference. Hatch is convinced that FINCA village banking is the answer to this need.

On a personal level, Hatch has sometimes found himself in difficult positions. In El Salvador, Nicaragua, and Peru, terrorists operate throughout the countryside, especially at night. On one evening in particular, Hatch and a group of campesinos crouched on the roof of a village building in the rain to escape marauding gunmen.

But the rewards, as Hatch himself says, far outweigh the risks. To poor villagers seeking to climb out of poverty, FINCA is considered an economic wonder cure—and the provider of the greatest opportunity of their lifetime.

Like so many of the other values in this book, opportunity plays an important role at Amway. We believe that each person is unique and should be able to reach their potential, whatever that is. As our business grows and becomes more successful, we are able to offer more and varied employment opportunities to the citizens of our community. And we try to find a place, not only for the physically impaired, but for people with mental challenges as well. We give them the opportunity to work to their best ability. This is a commitment of which we are very proud. We also consider our Amway Sales and Marketing Plan to be one of the best (if not *the* best) business opportunities in the world for individuals with a willingness to work but with limited capital to invest. It has allowed for an enormous range of success—success that is only limited by one's imagination and capacity for hard work. Ordinary people from New York to California, from China to Korea, from former Communist East Germany to Western Europe, and on every continent (with the exception of a *very* limited market in Antarctica) can find opportunity through the Amway business.

In America, opportunity and freedom are considered synonymous. We must preserve those rights by rediscovering and living America's values. We must continue to seek opportunity for ourselves and to provide opportunities for others. In so doing, we will contribute to their self-reliance, and to their freedom to realize their full potential.

## 23

# Education

I believe that we are all born with talents and abilities. We develop those abilities based upon what and how well we are taught. This is why education is so important, and why it tops the list of Americans' concerns. Not only does human progress depend upon education, but so does our freedom.

The truth is, opportunities will only be as good as our ability to take advantage of them, and this ability is largely determined by our level of education. By education, I don't just mean teaching math or physics, which, while important, are not my primary concern. I'm talking about teaching children the difference between right and wrong. This type of teaching is something that many people feel does not belong in the classroom. They believe that what is right for one person is not necessarily right for another and that no one person has the right to impose his or her values on others.

But I believe teaching basic values about our country's Judeo-Christian heritage is fundamental to understanding the very essence of our freedom.

When it is a question of personal freedom or collective freedom, I believe there *are* rights and wrongs about which we can't afford to disagree—particularly in America, where our birthright includes life, liberty, and the pursuit of happiness. Given that such values as honesty and reliability are essential to upholding freedom and that such values as work and accountability are important to our self-reliance and becoming free, it follows that it is important to teach those values and founding principles to our children.

As I have said, there is more to education than the three R's, computer literacy, or the teaching of geography. These subjects are important to our children's progress and future, as are the many new skills they will need to meet tomorrow's challenges. But it is rare to see a curriculum that includes courses about our American democratic heritage or about upholding freedom, integrity, self-reliance, or any of the other values discussed in this book. As I travel across our country, I hear many parents suggesting that our educators find ways to incorporate these lessons into everything they teach. I couldn't agree more!

Another important aspect of education is the importance of identifying teachers who inspire by example, living by the values they teach. Dick McMichael, the noon news anchor on WTVM-TV in Columbus, Georgia, would probably agree. McMichael was fortunate to have Bob Barr as a music teacher and bandleader. Barr taught his students not only musical technique but also how to be winners in life.

McMichael was a junior at the Jordan Vocational High

School in Columbus, Georgia, when he first met Bob Barr. A self-taught drummer, McMichael had volunteered to play the bass drum in his school's marching band. Barr had come to band practice to see if he would take the job as the band's director. To this day, McMichael doesn't know why Barr took the job. By some accounts the Jordan band was the worst high school band in the country. Not only were they lacking in technique—many of them didn't even know how to read music—but they came from a poor mill town that could afford neither good instruments nor a full-time director. That didn't seem to matter to Barr. He listened to the band as avidly as he might the New York Philharmonic. And when they were finished, he had something nice to say about practically everyone, including McMichael, who was praised for his ability to follow the other musicians.

Like many of the band members, Barr himself had little money when he was growing up. His father died when he was five. His mother worked as a hotel maid. When he was eight, an old Seminole Indian taught him to play the trumpet. A local bandmaster coached him on the tuba and then got him a scholarship to the Cincinnati Conservatory. While there, Barr won a national championship and then joined the Indianapolis Symphony. His true calling, however, was teaching. He considered the job at Jordan a welcome challenge.

The students loved Barr's enthusiasm. But it was his attitude that made a lasting difference. "You want to be a real band?" he asked them. "Then don't be satisfied until you're the best in the land. And you can be."

Barr communicated this message on many different levels. On one occasion he played them a recording of Beethoven's Ninth Symphony. He then explained that Beethoven was deaf when he wrote it. The fact that they weren't deaf gave them a huge advantage, he said. They had no excuse not to be the best.

Few Jordan students even dreamed of going to college or getting good jobs. Most expected to take their parents' places in the mills and factories in Columbus. But Barr had a different dream for them. At least for the time being. "If you want to be the best you can, it will mean giving it everything you have. Be here for practice tomorrow morning at eight a.m."

The next day was a Saturday, but he had the band members viewing practice on the weekend as an opportunity.

Barr and his wife, Anne, lived in a redbrick cottage that became a second home for the band members. In the morning, Anne would welcome them into her kitchen with smiles and pancakes.

McMichael remembers the day when Barr asked him to become the band's percussion leader. "The drum is the one instrument that I can't play," he told McMichael. "So you'll have to teach it for me."

Barr employed a method that great teachers have used for centuries: entrusting students with responsibilities and then guiding them in the process of meeting them.

McMichael remembers that year as the happiest of his young career. He taught percussion by staying one lesson ahead of his class. When he couldn't figure out a difficult passage, he would knock on Barr's office door. Often they talked a little about drumming and a lot about life.

A Barr rehearsal was something that his students didn't forget. When they reached their goals, he praised them with a smile or wink. When they failed, he took them to task.

Over a one-year period the band grew from seventeen to eighty-five, with Barr recruiting most of its members. Then he begged, borrowed, and requisitioned instruments. He visited his students' homes to work out ways for every member to stay in the band. He even arranged for loans for needy students. Eventually he persuaded the town to provide proper uniforms and a music room.

When band member John Henry didn't have $7.50 to buy white shoes to match his uniform, Barr gave him the shoes as a gift. If a band member didn't show up for rehearsal, Barr sent fellow students to find out why. He scheduled so many practices that students who had previously been troublemakers stopped getting into trouble. They just didn't have time; they were too busy trying to please their director-teacher.

Barr loved to plan halftime shows for Friday-night football games. On a typical Friday evening he could be found marching around on the hill above the field and shouting orders, running around attaching battery-powered lights to the musicians' shoes, or stuffing the smallest musician into an old bass drum for a surprise appearance at the show's end.

Four years after McMichael graduated, the Jordan Vocational High School band represented Georgia in a national competition in New York City and won first place. For a brief shining moment, Barr's band was the best in the land.

Barr has since died, and most of the band members no longer play instruments, but it shouldn't come as a surprise to anyone that Barr had a lasting effect on their lives. McMichael became a well-known newscaster, John Henry a decorated soldier. Percussionist Jim Fletcher teaches humanities and plays in the Columbus Symphony. Trumpeter Jimmy

Cross became chairman of the South Trust National Bank in Phenix City, Alabama. Larold Ragland became a bassoonist with the National Symphony Orchestra in Washington, D.C. And Rob George, whose trumpet skills were honed by Barr, went on to become chairman of Lummus Industries, the world's largest manufacturer of cotton gins.

Our schools, churches, synagogues, and other places of worship, and our youth organizations all play a role in educating our children in the principles of freedom. But there are an unlimited number of other ways for us to teach children the values that set us free. We can lead the way for others by being a good example, a good role model, or a good mentor.

Often, without our knowing it, others have identified us as people they look up to and want to model themselves after. Perhaps they have chosen us because they want to have what we have, because they admire the way we come across or handle ourselves, or because we have similar backgrounds. They may see our experiences as having given us a wisdom they could learn from, or our accomplishments as something they would like to emulate. These people—whether we know it or not, and whether we like it or not—look to us for guidance and direction on what decisions to make, how to respond to life's challenges, and even how to dress and act.

Imitation, as we have all heard, is the sincerest form of flattery. It is one of the primary and most natural modes of learning. As all parents should realize, their children will emulate their behavior. This prospect is sobering when we fully realize its implications. While it is encouraging to be assured that our good qualities will be emulated, it is also a reminder of our accountability that our faults and imperfections will be emulated as well. Therefore, we must consistently try to do what is right.

A child may make a role model out of practically anyone, from a teenager who lives down the street to a favorite teacher or a kindly uncle or aunt. Role models can be people we know and admire from a distance, or they can be great historical figures we read about in history books. For me, Jesus serves as my most important role model. My parents have also been very important examples to me through the years.

Today, many of our children's role models are television, film, and sports stars. Unfortunately, many of these figures do not realize the impact their lives have on children who choose to emulate them. Fortunately, there are many who do recognize the positive effect they can have on others by doing what is right.

A man who came to understand that, and learned to honor the responsibility that came with his fame and fortune, is Darrell Waltrip, the race car driver. He is a champion in more than one sense of the word, not just because of the many racing titles he has won, but because he has distinguished himself as an individual who cares about the kind of role model he presents to his fans. As Waltrip will be the first to admit, this wasn't always the case.

A few years ago race fans knew Waltrip as the "bad boy" of stock car racing, a driver who didn't care what people thought about him. Back then, the only thing that mattered was winning the race, and Waltrip had an uncanny ability to do just that.

Waltrip got started racing go-carts at the age of eight, and rose through the ranks, finally racing on the NASCAR circuit.

By age thirty-seven he had won over a million dollars in prize money and two back-to-back Winston Cup Championships.

"From Daytona to Talladega to Charlotte," Waltrip said, "I was the guy to beat."

Then, at the opening of a new season at the Daytona 500, he came screaming out of a turn at about two hundred miles an hour, only to face a stack-up of other cars directly in front of him. As he swerved to avoid a head-on collision, his car began to slide. He lost control, slammed into a retaining wall, bounced off a guardrail, and spun back across the track. It was a miracle he wasn't killed.

As happens with so many who have had a close brush with death, Waltrip began to question the person he had become and where he was going. He discovered that while he might have been leading a pack, he was not much of a leader, at least not for his wife, or for the thousands of fans across the country who watched his every move.

Subsequently, he set about making some major changes— changes that ultimately had a profound impact on his life, both at home and at the track. But just as important, they had an impact on the many young kids who had been modeling themselves after him.

One of the first things he did was to begin attending church regularly, eventually joining the church and renewing the spiritual dimension of his life. He began to take the steps needed to build a stable home environment for himself and his wife, Stevie. Within a year their first child, Jessica Leigh, was born, and a year after that, their daughter Sarah.

Fans recognized the change in Waltrip almost immediately. He now demonstrated compassion for his fellow drivers and showed courtesy and respect for the crowds in the bleachers. And although he had never expressly advocated drinking and driving, or the use of alcohol, he became increasingly aware of the fact that a beer company sponsored his race car.

His awareness was heightened even more when one day an irate mother pushed through the crowd of teenagers surrounding him and proceeded to lecture him about his image. "You ought to be ashamed of yourself," she said. "You're giving children the message that drinking, driving, and success go together."

She was right. The patches and insignias on his driver's suit said it all. He was a walking beer commercial.

It wasn't long before Waltrip left his old racing team and signed on with a new one—sponsored by a laundry detergent! When he eventually bought his own car, he was able to completely control which products he chose to promote. Waltrip also, among other things, played an instrumental role in establishing an outreach program that brings weekly Sunday morning chapel services to drivers and their families at racetracks across the country.

He can't say whether his subsequent victory at the Daytona 500 could be directly attributed to his new attitude on life, but he certainly felt a greater sense of accomplishment when he won NASCAR's most coveted trophy. He proved, not only for himself, but for his fans, that nice guys can finish first. His fans must have loved the great example he set because they voted him the most popular driver on the circuit.

While Darrell Waltrip is in a great position to be a role model to hundreds and even thousands, mentoring is perhaps even a more potent and effective teaching tool. Mentors do not have to be famous or even well known. They are often closer to home, working consciously with one or just a few "students." This is what mentoring is all about, as the mentor is able to monitor what he or she teaches and give direct feedback and relevant suggestions. Good mentors make themselves available over a long period of time. They are there to give good advice, to be an arm to lean on, or to do a little cheerleading, as the situation warrants. While being a good role model is important, it is necessary that we, as mentors, also work at a deeper level, truly investing in and impacting the lives of others.

Parents are in the best position to be mentors to their children. As you would have guessed by now, my father was my most important mentor. But I had other mentors too—Jay Van Andel; my father-in-law, Ed Prince; and Billy Zeoli, an ordained minister and close friend of my father. From each of them I learned something different, whether it was how to communicate more effectively, how to stop and think before I act, to have the courage to do what is right, or just plain old street smarts.

I also feel honored to be considered a mentor by my younger brother Doug. When I was in my late teens and he was playing junior league football, I was able to be his coach for a number of years. That experience cemented our relationship. Now, years later, as we work together professionally, he still looks to me for occasional "coaching."

Mentors are found within families and outside them. For David Belton, a happily married father of three and a successful Columbia, South Carolina, attorney, his mother and five sisters played a very important part in his youth. But it was Billy Thomas, a bowlegged man of small stature and quiet demeanor—a staff member at the Mount Vernon Southside

Boys Club—who truly became his mentor. David and his sisters, supported by their mother, who worked hard as a cleaning lady, grew up in a housing project just outside of New York City. If a boy was to learn anything in the projects, it was about the world of drugs and crime.

This was not to be the case with David. When he was six years old his mother took him down to the Boys Club. As David likes to say, "I went in as a young boy and came out a young man." The Boys Club was right on the way home from school and impossible to avoid, so David and many other neighborhood boys would stop by every day. They went because it was a place to go, a place to play games and sports with each other. Little did they know that Billy Thomas and his fellow staff had much more on their agenda. They were there to teach the boys values and skills. But not just the skills it took to play basketball, Ping-Pong, or chess; they wanted to impart the skills it took to succeed in life.

In looking back, David realizes that one of the most important elements of his experience was that Billy was there for the boys, day after day and year after year. He was in it for the long haul. Thus Billy could teach about responsibility one day and refer back to something that he and the boys did or talked about two years or even five years before.

Billy wasn't one of those guys who would come in for an hour and lecture with slogans like "Just say no." As the boys matured and became more capable of understanding what he was trying to teach them, he sometimes referred back to an incident over and over again—until the message sunk in.

In Billy, David saw consistency and commitment in action. Billy taught David and his friends as they played games and took on the challenges he gave them. Often Billy would give them titles and roles to play in an effort to teach them responsibility. If they messed up, he'd swiftly remove the title and all the benefits that came with it. But his message wasn't that the boys were no good—the message was that they weren't ready yet.

But the tolerance level for misbehavior was pretty low. Here was truly a case of "tough love." The boys at the club were taught to live by the honor system, and if someone cheated, the rest were told that they had no reason to cheat as well. When this made David angry, Billy told him that there would always be someone out there who was going to cheat to win and that he would just have to work harder and smarter. "No matter what happens, no matter what others do to you, turn it around and make the most of it." Billy always reminded them, "Don't get mad. Just get stronger and more determined. Be so darn good that no one can stop you from doing anything."

This was advice that David took to heart, applying it at some of the most crucial turning points in his life, whether it was getting that science credit he needed to graduate from high school or passing the bar exams in South Carolina. David believes that what he gained from his years with Billy Thomas at the Boys Club made such a difference in his life that he doesn't just *want* to carry on in like tradition, but is obligated to.

Thirty years later, David is now a national board trustee of the current Boys and Girls Club, an organization that serves 5.5 million children. He also serves as chairman of the Boys and Girls Club of the Midlands in Columbia, South Carolina. A part of Billy Thomas lives on in David and will live on in his own children and the children he serves at the club and for generations to come. As David points out, while other kinds of gifts are important, no others leave the kind of legacy that a mentor like Billy Thomas does.

As stated earlier, mentorship is one of the most potent and effective tools of education because it so dramatically impacts others. As I demonstrated here, a mentor does not need to have power and position to be effective.

While our children are clearly in need of education, adults can also benefit from learning. And it *is* possible to educate and foster integrity, self-reliance, and ability among the members of our community's most needy. Bob Coté, who operates an innovative program for the homeless and destitute in Denver, has given this subject a great deal of thought, for he was once one of his city's most needy. His philosophy is a simple but powerful one: a hand up, not a handout.

At six foot three and 240 pounds, Bob Coté has an imposing presence, which comes in handy living and working in the rougher neighborhoods of Denver, Colorado. He was an athletic youth from the streets of Detroit, a boxer who competed in the Golden Gloves competition. As a young adult, he went into sales, which, as it turned out, was a successful field for him. Several years later, he relocated to Denver to be with a girlfriend and started a successful lawn maintenance company there.

But his success was short-lived. When he and his girlfriend broke up, Bob went into a tailspin. What once had been just a social drinking problem began to take over his life, rendering him destitute within a year. Because of his alcoholism, he became totally isolated, eventually landing in the skid row district of Denver. Still, he managed to fool himself into thinking that he didn't have a serious problem, at least compared with the other residents around him.

It was a simple realization that finally turned Bob Coté around. One afternoon, he saw a fellow skid row denizen, Billy Palmer, passed out on the sidewalk. Palmer, Coté knew, had once been an educated man from a comfortable home. Now he was a homeless alcoholic. Like a thunderbolt, it struck Coté that it was only time that separated him from the man at his feet. That was, unless he changed something. Coté emptied his bottle of vodka onto the sidewalk and decided on the spot to stop drinking forever.

Newly sober, Coté took up residence in a run-down storefront on Larimer Street. He wanted out of his situation and he wanted to bring others out with him. It took Coté two months of observing the behavior of the nine other alcoholics and drug abusers who lived there before a plan of action solidified in his mind. Offering a way out of their predicament, Coté organized the men into what became an organization called Step 13. Many people wrongfully assume that Coté named this after the Alcoholics Anonymous famous 12-step program. The real inspiration has a different origin. Coté points out that Jesus and His disciples numbered 13 and that there are 13 stripes on the American flag. Cote's intent was to reach out to those substance abusers who had already tried and failed in other programs, and who had nowhere else to go but to their graves. Most important, it was to be run *by* and *for* the substance abusers themselves.

The rules of "Step," as it is called on the street, are simple: no drugs, no alcohol, and participants must actively try to find jobs. A bed is a privilege, and leaving it unmade is a good way to lose it. Attendance at Alcoholics Anonymous meetings is required twice a week, and anyone who uses one of the forbidden substances will be shown the door. Breath and urine tests are given every day.

The most striking departure Step 13 makes from the typical shelter program is that Coté requires the participants to take responsibility for themselves rather than be lulled into dependency by generous but destructive indulgences such as meals cooked and served for them. He had discovered the hard way that handouts such as these just reinforced feelings of dependency. No such free ride is offered at Step 13. Residents are charged five dollars per day rent, and everyone cooks for themselves. The message is clear: "You are perfectly capable of caring for yourself."

Of the first nine participants, some succeeded, and some failed. Some left but then returned. Then others began to come, looking for the hope that Coté's program offered. Detoxification and law enforcement programs began referring offenders. The most notable success story was a man who had worn out his welcome in at least forty different detox facilities. Coté laid down the law but sheltered the man until he found work, first washing dishes, then doing odd jobs in maintenance. That man, Jack Williams, is now a successful and prosperous contractor. But he hasn't forgotten where he has been. He hires his workers from Coté's program.

Remarkably, Step 13 has never accepted government funding of any sort, nor has it sought any. Coté remains suspicious of those who rely on such resources and considers many of the programs that operate on those funds "hooked" on taxpayer money.

Instead, Coté depends upon private gifts and what certainly appears to be divine providence. One such case involved a physician who was discovered drunk but unhurt in his wrecked car, which had jumped the curb. The physician was without money or identification but refused to stay at Step 13. Coté got him checked into a local motel and paid for the room himself. Before he left the doctor, Coté gave him one of his cards. Years later, a check arrived for $10,000, seemingly out of the blue. The doctor had recently died and had bequeathed the money to Coté's program. Such "miracles" continue to happen, and Step 13's doors remain open.

Coté strongly contends that the vast majority of panhandlers on the street who ask for money to buy a meal are not, in fact, interested in getting food. Rather, they're interested in feeding their drug or alcohol habit. To prove this, he printed meal tickets with the message "Good for One Free Meal." The tickets also offered a job, a place to live, and a means of taking charge of one's life. Step 13's address was included. Approximately ninety thousand of these meal tickets were distributed over a period of five years, yet only two dozen of the individuals who received the cards showed up at the Step 13 shelter to take the offer. Of those twenty-four, not one agreed to take a job or enter Coté's program.

There is, in fact, an ever-growing body of evidence to suggest that the main problem behind homelessness is not poverty but substance abuse. This is not a popular message with many homeless advocates. Attempts at tracking the homeless, a move Coté feels is necessary, have been defeated via a number of methods, including challenges on constitutional grounds. But Coté persists. He's convinced that there is a pressing need to create a national database. He feels that unless and until reliable data are collected and the true cause of homelessness is understood, there will be no way to honestly or accurately attack the problem of homelessness itself.

Database or not, Step 13 continues to illuminate the route to self-reliance and freedom for the homeless citizens of Denver. In the dozen or more years of its existence, more than two thousand individuals have passed through its doors. Coté claims that about a third have made lasting changes in their lives, becoming sober and productive citizens as a direct result of his no-nonsense challenge: "If you screw up, you're out of here. But if you're serious about changing your life, I'll help you any way I can."

As all these stories demonstrate, the importance of education cannot be underestimated. Ultimately the extent of our success in educating our children in knowing right from wrong, in upholding freedom, and in becoming free will determine whether we *remain* "the land of the free."

## ✌ 24 ✌

# Brotherhood

When our founding fathers, in the Declaration of Independence, declared that "all men are created equal," they were not referring just to "men," but to all citizens. As discussed earlier, our founders also understood that we are called to practice the "brotherly" love Jesus referred to when he called us to "love our neighbor as ourselves." It seems appropriate, then, that the official beginning of our great nation was signed into being in Philadelphia, "the city of brotherly love."

I close this book with a discussion of brotherhood, because brotherhood ties together all of the values discussed previously. Without brotherhood, we cannot achieve true honesty, true compassion, or true commitment; without brotherhood, we cannot implement charity, service, or leadership. In order to uphold freedom, become free, and preserve freedom, we must practice brotherhood, reconciling the differences between us.

To me, brotherhood not only means honoring the freedom and rights of every man and woman regardless of their ethnic origins, skin color, the language they speak, or the religion they practice, but it also requires supporting each other, getting to know one another, and establishing relationships, so we can better understand and respect one another.

Every person has their humanity in common, as we are "one in His creation." It is a fact we can neither change nor deny. There is a great deal of variety within the human race, but we don't have to lose our distinctiveness to get along. The more we look for and discover similarities between ourselves and others, respecting our differences, the more encompassing and expansive become our feelings of compassion. If we respect the humanity in each other and allow each other the human dignity that is our birthright, then no matter what our differences, shalom, civility, and true brotherhood will be ours.

In this age of information highways, supersonic travel, and international news networks, the opportunity for expanding brotherhood has never been greater, nor has it ever been so important. We can watch events on the other side of our city, state, country, or planet unfold on our television screens even as they are taking place. At no time in the history of man has it been possible for so many people to share their hopes, aspirations, and feelings with so many others.

Unfortunately, today there is some confusion in regard to the notion of brotherhood. Many people think that embracing brotherhood means changing our own standards to accommodate those of others, or letting go of our patriotism or abandoning our own national interests. However, embracing brotherhood doesn't mean giving up what we believe in. It means upholding what we believe in without apology and accepting others' right to do the same.

In my opinion, brotherhood is the grandest vision of all—one that our nation of great diversity must continually strive toward. A great example of the spirit of brotherhood was evidenced between Francis Aebi and his neighbor, Tamaki Ninomiya, two rose farmers from outside Richmond, in northern California. Their story began in the dark days of World War II, when California, like much of the rest of the country, was caught in the tide of fear and the resulting racism that led to thousands of Japanese Americans being deprived of their freedom and property and being detained in internment camps.

Francis was of Swiss descent. Tamaki was Japanese. By the start of World War II, each family had become modestly successful selling their flowers in San Francisco. They each had nice homes, well-cared-for greenhouses, and seven children between them. Roses from both farms had earned well-deserved reputations for their long vase-life.

While the bombing of Pearl Harbor on December 7, 1941, changed the lives of all Americans, for Japanese Americans living in California, the war meant strong sanctions, unpredictable reactions, and even imprisonment.

In Contra Costa County, where the Aebis and the Ninomiyas had their farms, the news was grim. Rumors circulated that a car owned by a Japanese had been overturned on Route 17, and that a greenhouse owned by a Japanese farmer had been vandalized. Finally rumors spread that soon Japanese people were to be rounded up and sent off to internment camps.

As the situation became tense, Francis appeared at Tamaki's house. He made it clear that if the need arose, Tamaki could count on him to look after his property.

Ten weeks after the bombing at Pearl Harbor, President Franklin Roosevelt signed into law the executive order that designated military areas from which any or all persons could be excluded. This was the order that ultimately resulted in 120,000 Japanese being physically removed from their homes in California and relocated to camps.

It was now Tamaki's turn to visit Francis. He arrived carrying the family's most valuable possession, an ornamental Japanese doll dressed in an elaborate costume of black and white silk, housed in a glass case. Tamaki offered it to Francis as a gift.

Francis made it clear that he wasn't going to accept the doll as a gift. But he did agree to hold on to it for the Ninomiyas "until things get back to normal."

A month later, Tamaki arrived again. This time he handed Francis his bank book.

At noon on a cold February day, less than a month later, a black sedan pulled up to the Ninomiyas' home. Four men dressed in business suits got out, escorted Tamaki into the car, and took him away, with only the work clothes on his back.

That same day, Tamaki's pregnant wife and their five children went to stay with friends in Livingston, in central California, where they hoped to avoid the same fate as Tamaki. They loaded their pickup truck with clothes, a few pots and pans, and some favorite toys, and drove away from the home that Tamaki's father had built with his own hands.

The town of Livingston offered Tamaki's wife and children no protection. With the signing of the civilian exclusion order, all persons of Japanese ancestry, citizens included, were to be evacuated from the area. Evacuees were required to carry with them bedding, clothing, and table articles that included a bowl for each member of the family.

Three months later, the Ninomiyas were sent to Granada, Colorado, along with hundreds of other Japanese families. They were assigned to wooden barracks covered with tar paper and surrounded by barbed wire. Armed guards monitored their movements.

Many people might have been tempted to let their competitor's nursery go bankrupt. Not so Francis Aebi. He decided to do everything he could to keep both his own and his neighbor's nursery running. In fact, he not only kept the Ninomiya nursery operating; he did the same for the Kawai and Sugihara nurseries.

This added responsibility was an overwhelming proposition, but the long hours and grueling labor weren't the only hardships. Another was the rationing of fuel. To qualify for a farmer's ration of fuel, Francis had to raise vegetables. His lovely roses had to be cleared away to make room for cucumbers and tomatoes if he was to save his nursery. He began by clearing his own property. Eventually he had to clear both the Tamaki and Kawai nurseries. Nonetheless, he managed to save a few choice rosebushes.

Months turned into years. The whole Aebi family now had to labor with Francis to keep the nurseries operating. The children worked in the greenhouses before school and on weekends. Francis himself put in eighteen-hour days. He couldn't hire help because there was barely enough money from the produce to put food on his own table, not to mention the fear that news of what he was doing would invite recrimination.

During the next two years, the only news from the internment camps was that Tamaki had been allowed to rejoin his family in Granada, and to meet, for the first time, his new infant son.

Francis, his wife, and their two children continued their exhausting labor, facing new challenges as gardening supplies became increasingly scarce. His son, however, had finally turned sixteen and could now be counted on to help drive their produce into market.

At long last the war ended. Word came across the public-address system in the relocation-center cafeteria that the detainees were going home. They boarded trucks, and then were transported to northern California by train.

In his letters, Francis had reported that all was well at the Ninomiya nursery. Yet it was only natural for Tamaki to wonder if this could possibly be true. Many Japanese Americans returned to find their homes burned down or their property looted. At the very least, they knew their homes would be in terrible disrepair.

When the train carrying the Ninomiya family arrived in Richmond, the Aebis were waiting on the platform. Both Francis and Tamaki were so thin and drawn from the last three years that they barely recognized each other.

The Ninomiyas piled their pots and pans into the Aebis' truck and excitedly started for home. Within a short time they were turning off Route 17 and pulling into their driveway. Tamaki got out, followed by his children and his father, Jiro.

Tamaki's first revelation was that his nursery was exactly as he had left it three years before, only now there were cucumbers and other vegetables growing along with the roses. Not a single pane of glass was missing from the greenhouse. And the glass was so clean that it sparkled in the sunlight.

Inside the Ninomiyas' home, the family's possessions were just where they had left them, and the Japanese silk doll was back in its place. A single rose sat in a bud vase on the kitchen counter. Nearby was the Ninomiyas' bank passbook, including the deposits that Francis had been able to make from selling Tamaki's roses at the San Francisco flower market.

Tamaki shook Francis's hand and thanked his neighbor from the bottom of his heart, as did the Kawai and Sugihara families when they returned to similar situations.

Francis, now eighty-six, is still growing roses, as are his grandchildren, and as are the grandchildren of his Japanese neighbors. His act of brotherhood and compassion, like his rosebushes, produced beautiful results.

Brotherhood often requires more than just plain neighborliness. It requires cooperation, communication, and courage. A unique and inspiring story demonstrating this kind of brotherhood took place in my home state of Michigan, in the city of Ann Arbor, where a synagogue and a church have teamed up to share the same building. How that came about is as inspiring as what happened when they did.

The first overture was made by the newly founded Reformed Jewish congregation, Temple Beth Emeth. Their problem was a simple one. They had no place to meet for their Friday night services, and no money to build a temple. That was when they decided to approach another congregation, the St. Clare of Assisi Episcopal Church, in the hopes that the church might agree to rent them the use of their meeting hall.

"There had been informal events between our two congregations before," reminisced the Reverend Douglas Evett, who was in on the plan from the outset. "We had done a seder dinner together. Their rabbi and our rector had also taught a class together. Also, some personal relationships had formed between the laypeople of the two congregations."

A committee was formed to explore the possibilities. The financial contribution Beth Emeth offered was equal to a substantial one-seventh of the parish's total operating budget, and since the Jewish services and Christian services were to be held at different times, it seemed a natural match. While the idea seemed to meet short-term practical needs, the historical differences between Jews and Christians were a hurdle no one was certain could be surmounted. There was only one way to find out.

"At that time, we had probably a hundred and fifty or so parishioners at St. Clare, and Beth Emeth had about a hundred in their congregation," the Reverend Evett remembers. "Losing even one family represented a big loss" to either congregation.

Things went along well for the first few years. The Beth Emeth congregation made steady contributions to their new building fund, bringing them ever closer to the day they could build their own temple. The St. Clare congregation went about their business as usual. The offices of the two congregations were in separate locations, so the two parties rarely met or had significant dealings with one another.

Then along came the Yom Kippur War. Jewish congregations across the country were donating funds to support Israel. In a generous show of support, Temple Beth Emeth donated nearly all of the funds they had earmarked for the new building.

Evett remembers well a conversation with Rabbi Bruce Warshaw. "Bruce told me they were going to have to start all over again from scratch. I said, almost offhandedly, 'Why don't you just stay?' He looked at me the way you look at someone who's made an utterly preposterous suggestion, and said, 'Well, gee, maybe we ought to.' "

Evett, Rabbi Warshaw, the synagogue's president, and the senior warden of the parish decided to meet to explore the realities and challenges of such a permanent arrangement.

"It solved a number of problems on the spot," said Evett recently, "which on the surface were purely practical, but were also, in some sense, compelling for both congregations."

Once the committee of four had established that it was an idea worth pursuing, a committee drawn from the members of the two congregations was established to set up a contractual agreement and bylaws.

"What that did was effectively widen the circle of people involved in the process," recalls Evett. "And out of that grew a natural process by which, in the course of things, we had occasion to meet, see, and talk to each other."

As a part of the agreement, Temple Beth Emeth was allocated space in the church offices, and the two congregations even shared a secretary.

"After that, members of the synagogue were always in the church's offices, and church members were always in the synagogue's offices," says Evett.

The process continued its dynamic growth. Out of the committee that drafted the corporation grew another committee whose specific purpose was to encourage dialogue between the two congregations, further cementing the relationship and providing an opportunity for the two groups to discover and explore their shared interests and goals.

Recognizing the possibility of conflict arising out of the differences between the two faiths, they devised a mechanism for negotiating and resolving any such discord. It was in the form of a committee, which they named the Interfaith Resolution Council. However, since both congregations have always had an active desire to resolve any discord before it comes to loggerheads, it comes as no surprise that in the years since its formation, the Interfaith Resolution Council has never formally met.

Instead of conflict, there have been a number of cooperative ventures over the years that have taken advantage of the two faiths' unique qualities and conventions, including their religious calendars. For example, on Yom Kippur and Rosh Hashanah, Christian parishioners take over baby-sitting duties, so that no Jewish parents will have to miss the High Holy Day services. Reciprocally, Jewish parents take over baby-sitting duties for Christian parents on Easter and Christmas.

Another sign that the union has worked well for all parties is the fact that today, St. Clare of Assisi Episcopal has a membership of over 225 and temple Beth Emeth boasts a membership in excess of 400.

But vitally important to all concerned, each congregation

follows the teachings of its own faith without trying to mix with or challenge the basic tenets of the others. Prominently displayed in front of the church/synagogue stand a cross and a Star of David. Together, they symbolize the possibilities inherent in mutual respect and a shared love of God. Those symbols standing together also bear witness to the vital and ongoing spirit of brotherhood that is born of goodwill and the love of our neighbor.

The Christian concept of "love thy neighbor as thyself" speaks clearly to the idea of brotherhood. Jesus taught that there was only one commandment that came before this, and that was "love God with all your heart, soul, mind, and strength." He also taught that we are to be our "brother's keeper"—for we were all created in the image of God and we are all one under God. Our nation's great seal echoes this. On it we find "E Pluribus Unum," which means "from many, one."

Although the civil rights and other social activist movements have successfully brought about changes to our culture, they have failed to inspire our nation to move beyond integration to reconciliation. As authors Spencer Perkins and Chris Rice point out in their important book *More Than Equals*, "Civil rights is a political concept; the brotherhood spoken of by biblical and contemporary prophets is a much higher calling. It is spiritual and must be approached spiritually." In order to do what is right, "loving our neighbor as ourselves," we must begin reconciling the differences between us.

Brotherhood is not only essential to solving problems in our country, it's essential to solving serious world problems and supporting human progress. As long as people are unwilling or unable to feel compassion for their neighbors, as long as human rights are not recognized and upheld, and as long as people demonize others, there will be armed conflicts, people will die of unchecked disease and starvation, and millions will live under tyranny.

I end this book with brotherhood because I believe that until the spirit of brotherhood is fully realized in our nation and throughout the world—until everyone on earth takes on the responsibility of upholding the rights of their fellow human beings—we will not be fully free. Brotherhood calls for compassion on a grand scale—compassion that guides us to do what is right for the right reasons.

As the people of a country built on the foundation of human rights and freedom for all, Americans can and must provide leadership in this universal quest for brotherhood. Americans should take the lead and teach the true value of freedom to all the people of the earth by setting the example.

The more we uphold the rights and freedom that our nation stands for, the more likely the rest of the world will come to recognize the importance of these values and then secure the same rights and freedom for themselves. By maintaining a high level of integrity, self-reliance, and brotherhood everywhere we travel, Americans can show the rest of the world how true freedom elevates the human experience, not only spiritually, but emotionally and materially. And we will remain, as President Reagan said, "a shining city on a hill."

Let this be our common vision for the future.

# Conclusion

Individuals and families have been streaming to the shores of America for over two centuries, searching for freedom and all that freedom provides. Indeed, America's greatest struggles have been either to bring about more freedom or to protect the freedoms we already have. Early colonists faced the dangers of treacherous and unknown seas, scurvy, and other diseases to make their way to America. They came to be free of the shackles of tyranny and to enjoy religious freedom. Our founding fathers risked life and limb when they wrote and signed the Declaration of Independence, a document that changed the world. The American Revolution brought about freedom from the oppression of the ruling classes and the excessive taxation that supported them. Our Constitution, another remarkable document, was designed expressly to protect the freedom and rights of our nation's citizens. Later generations fought on every front to abolish slavery and to honor the equal rights of all citizens.

As I conclude this book, I am reminded of the words engraved on the Statue of Liberty: "Give me your tired, your poor, Your huddled masses, yearning to be free, The wretched refuse of your teeming shore, Send these, the homeless, tempest tost to me: I lift my lamp beside the golden door."

America and the values on which it was founded are the "golden door." But I am gravely concerned that the "door" has been tarnished by the efforts of some to define freedom as doing what we want without being accountable. As I have emphasized throughout this book, freedom does not come from just doing what we want; freedom also requires doing what is right. Upholding freedom takes honesty, reliability, fairness, compassion, courage, humility, reason, and a great deal of self-discipline. Becoming free is not easy. It requires optimism, commitment, initiative, work, perseverance, accountability, cooperation, and stewardship. And preserving freedom demands personal commitment from each of us. It requires encouragement, forgiveness, service, charity, leadership, opportunity, education, and brotherhood.

Early Americans fought hard for their freedom. Today's citizens must fight hard as well. In many ways our battle is on a different front. It is a fight to preserve the very fabric of our society, and it is a fight that cannot be won on the floor of our legislatures or be resolved by our lawmakers. It must be fought by each and every one of us. It is a battle that must first be won in our hearts and minds, and then in our homes, our schools, our workplaces, our places of worship, and our communities.

Although I continue to be optimistic about the future of our great land and our virtually unlimited potential to lead the peoples of the world in the right direction, I do believe that we are facing a crisis of character that threatens the fundamental integrity of our nation. If we want the next generation of Americans to have the freedom our forefathers intended, then we must teach them, by example, to "do what is right." We must provide our children, the youth who will serve as our leaders in the new millennium, with the proper foundation; we must teach them the importance of the values that make freedom possible.

For this reason, I challenge all who read this to rediscover our American values. Be bold. Take the first step today. Smile at someone. Be humble in your achievements. Work hard. Send a note of appreciation to a friend or colleague. Volunteer to help in your community. Tutor a child. Be someone's big brother or big sister. The list of opportunities is endless. The important thing is that you make the effort and follow through on your commitment.

I am an eternal optimist, I know we can put the shine back on the "golden door." And the luster it provides will once again be the beacon for all who seek freedom.

It is a dream and conviction of mine to preserve the dreams of those who came before us . . . to protect freedom in this "promised land." It is my hope and prayer that, after you read this book, this will become your dream and conviction as well. As President Ronald Reagan said so eloquently in his first inaugural address: "We have every right to dream heroic dreams . . . to believe in ourselves . . . in our capacity to perform great deeds, to believe that together with God's help we can and will resolve the problems which now confront us . . . and, after all, why shouldn't we believe that? We are Americans."

# Acknowledgments

I have learned through the writing of this book what a tremendous undertaking the writing and publishing process can be. There is no way I could have accomplished the task without the help and assistance of my very trusted family, friends, and colleagues.

First and foremost, I want to thank my parents, Rich and Helen DeVos. The values that I presented in this book, I learned from them. They definitely taught me the value of doing the right thing, and for that I am forever grateful. I also thank my wife, Betsy, for her input in this book and for the excellent help she provided in the editing process.

A special thanks goes to Billy Zeoli, a dear friend and mentor. Billy was insistent that I take the time to write this book, and thanks to his continuous encouragement and guidance, I was successful in accomplishing the task. I hope he is as proud of the result as I am.

My editor, Arnold Dolin, definitely deserves an award for his patience. He was always there to assist me as we went through the tedious editing process, even up to the last minute. In addition, my agent, Alan Nevins, made sure all the details of the writing process were coordinated; without his help this book would have never been possible.

There were also many people who helped me get my thoughts and ideas in proper form for this book. They include Sidney Kirkpatrick, Nancy Webster-Thurlbeck, Bill Payne, Judith Markham, Neil Plantinga, Father Robert Sirico, Rabbi Daniel Lapin, Jeff Sikkenga, Scott Gordon, and Gregory Gronbacher.

I also want to thank the people whose stories are profiled. They are the real heroes for they are living the values that are the "Foundations of Our Freedom for the 21st Century." They include: the Aebi and Ninomiya families of Contra Costa County, John Beal, David Belton, John Byrd, Andy and Phyllis Chelsea, Bob Cote, Kelly and Dale Clem, Warren and Judy Davis, Ron Dennis, Fay Durant, David and Falaka Fattah, Jeremy Finch, Willie Gary, Robert George, Eula Hall, John Hatch, Dr. Robert Hickman, John Jeavons, Roger Johnson, Arthur Kaplan, James Kearney, Bill Kellogg, Mike Krzyzewski, Charles McClure, Dick McMichael, Jerry Mercer, Thomas Monaghan, Jim Munsey, Joy and Danny Murray, William Pagonis, Bessie Pender, Judy Petrucci, Gary and Corrie Lynne Player, Janice Robertson, Stephen Reed, Nancy Rhodes, Gene Spanos, John Stanford, Linda Stillman, Dr. Kenneth Swan, Darrell Waltrip, and Denny Whelan.

# Index